COMMIT TO WHAT IS

A GUIDED WORKBOOK FOR BUILDING A REVOLUTIONARY RELATIONSHIP WITH OUR EMOTIONS AND OURSELVES

Commit To What Is:
A guided workbook for building a revolutionary relationship with our emotions and ourselves

Copyright © 2021 Susan Kullman
Published by Mystery School Press
An imprint of Emergence Education

ISBN: 978-1-7358111-2-3

Mystery School Press
P.O. Box 63767
Philadelphia, PA 19147
mysteryschoolpress.com

Cover design by Silvia Rodrigues
Cover art by Louis Parsons (louisparsonsart.com)

COMMIT
TO
WHAT
IS

A GUIDED WORKBOOK FOR BUILDING A
REVOLUTIONARY RELATIONSHIP
WITH OUR EMOTIONS & OURSELVES

Susan Kullman

MYSTERY SCHOOL PRESS

Philadelphia, Pennsylvania

Susan Kullman

ACKNOWLEDGEMENTS

I must thank the Spirit that resides within me, ultimately the largest guiding system I have for bringing forth this work.

I have many support systems in my life that have enabled me to create this work, namely my beautiful husband Michael and son Jack, whose love and energy nourish me. I have been blessed with wonderful family, friends, and students, all of whom hold a very special place in my heart.

I am extremely grateful for the many wonderful teachers and coaches, namely Nina Gomes, Nevine Michaan, Liz Koch, and Marc David, who have graciously handed down their knowledge, insights, and experience to me.

I would especially like to thank my mentor and friend, Jeff Carreira for having the faith and trust to support my work. His presence in my life is a gift.

Lastly, I would like to thank Faryn Sand, who helped compile and organize this material into a digestible form. Her knowledge and support truly made this book possible.

Susan Kullman

CONTENTS

Susan Kullman

INTRODUCTION

Susan Kullman

WELCOME. THE FOLLOWING PAGES CONTAIN my life's work, a body of knowledge I discovered during the course of my own twenty-five-year journey of self-growth and transformation. My deep hope is that this work will serve you as profoundly as it has served me.

As early as I can remember, I felt as if my emotions uncontrollably impacted every aspect of my life. I remember going to bed each night wondering what kind of mood I would experience upon waking the next day; I never trusted that I would accomplish what I wanted to, as it seemed to me that my emotions controlled my life and everything in it.

I could feel my heart's profound desires, and even knew what I wanted to create, yet I simultaneously experienced a constant sense of powerlessness. I worried that I would never be able to manifest anything worthwhile as long as I felt controlled by the erratic nature of my emotional world, for I knew that this way of being and experiencing life could never lend itself to consistency or, ultimately, to progress.

In the mainstream medical world, I was given a list of various titles, terms, and suggested medications that correlated to my experience of emotional dysregulation. To be clear, I am in no way suggesting that for some, this isn't a necessary route to stability and wellbeing, or at least a pivotal support along the way. For me personally, though, there was also a voice within that never wanted solely to accept these titles and mainstream solutions as the only possible lens or resolution for my growth and healing—nor did I want to accept, however, the feelings of weakness and insecurity that my emotions so often created. My journey felt endless and daunting.

Then, something pivotal happened. Namely, my entire inner world changed when I learned the notion of, and began practicing ceaselessly, the art and science of shifting my relationship with my own emotions.

I feel compelled to share this work with you in an effort not only to provide you with a sense of hope about the very real potential for your own emotional empowerment and freedom, but also to share the tools, practices and theories that support this work of *shifting our relationships to our own emotions.*

The gift that this work has given me goes far beyond a heightened ability to fully own and direct my life. For me, shifting the way that I relate to my emotions has also proven to be the most effective route to achieving true emotional intimacy within, self-compassion, and the knowledge that I can truly manifest anything that my heart desires.

What generates this new, ideal brand of relationship with ourselves—according to my own lifelong practice, as well as decades of coaching others in this work—is the ability to truly *relax into* our feelings. To experience them without the need to justify, analyze, defend, stagnate in, or hold onto any one emotional state. This new relationship with our emotions is one that offers a sense of coming home to oneself with greater vulnerability (read: *power*). This deeper connection with ourselves then organically generates deeper connection with others, and in fact, with all of life.

Cultivating this level of authenticity and trust with our own emotions can also very often help alleviate self-judgment, and therefore, the judgment we place on others. It is my hope that we, as a society, truly begin to understand the options that are available to us regarding how to navigate our emotional responses when it comes to relating to ourselves and to others. The ways that we have been unconsciously programmed by the dominant culture to act, speak, and respond based upon our emotions, are not our only options; there are other things we can do, and other ways we can be, that ultimately lead to our own growth and transformation.

In the pages forthcoming, we will explore how shifting your relationship with your own emotions is paramount in order to transcend previously perceived limitations and self-limiting beliefs. You will have the opportunity to achieve a deeper sense of self, to learn how to release negative belief patterns, and truly, as trite as it may sound, to cultivate the ability to manifest anything that your heart desires.

Shifting your relationship with your own emotions is one of the most effective ways to evolve, for it helps release old and limiting self-identity in exchange for positive behavioral shifts and newly elevated personal potential.

This workbook serves as both an informative text and an experiential guide. Specifically, the purpose of this information and the exercises provided here is to help you adopt a more objective perspective when it comes to your relationship with your own emotions.

A healthy level of objectivity often gives way to heightened states of awareness by offering a space from which to more effectively dissolve emotional blocks that otherwise hinder our way forward toward positive action and aligned manifestation; these emotional blocks are what typically stand between *knowing* what we need to do in order to transform, and *doing* what we need to do in order to transform.

When we create a healthy level of objectivity to dissolve these blocks, our newly heightened awareness then gives way to the release of outdated and overly rigid personal patterns and habits. And because objectivity helps eradicate the intense self-judgment that many of us carry, the theories and practices offered here will also support you in the cultivation of deeper self-understanding and, perhaps most importantly, self-compassion.

Creating a new relationship with your emotions, and therefore with yourself—one that is both objective and truly compassionate—can ultimately enhance your capacity to embody a new way of living.

To learn to allow yourself to *fully feel what you feel* without fear, shame, self-judgment, or our often resulting tendencies of suppression and avoidance, is nothing short of life-changing.

This is true both in terms of how we feel and, therefore, show up in our lives, as well as in the forging of new neurological pathways that occurs whenever we release an old habit or form a new one. And indeed, the way we relate to our emotions is absolutely a product of habit, a concept we will explore in greater detail in the coming chapters.

Generally speaking, when we suppress our emotions, we utilize an important store of energy in order to do so, and conversely, when we allow ourselves to fully experience our emotions, we release the emotional, psychological, and physical burden that arises when we try to block or avoid them. Our energy is therefore no longer consumed with this task, and is instead free for us to use in other healthier ways, moving us further along a trajectory of heightened clarity and balance.

There are many reasons for our human tendency to suppress or avoid uncomfortable emotions, ones we will explore in depth in this workbook. By familiarizing yourself with this tendency itself, as well as the reasons behind it, you will increase your self-awareness, and thereby empower yourself to make a new set of choices regarding your relationship with your own emotions.

You will learn to sit with yourself in a space of emotional vulnerability, to shed detrimental defenses, to become emotionally intimate with the different layers of your own consciousness, to move through those layers towards greater authenticity, and ultimately, to become your own best friend.

Learning to become comfortable with uncomfortable emotions requires both commitment and practice since, as mentioned, it entails forging an entirely new qualitative and neurophysiological relationship to them, and to yourself. And it is in the cultivation of that more authentic and courageously vulnerable relationship, that you will position yourself to experience your true personal power and potential.

HOW TO USE THIS WORKBOOK

Because this workbook is intended to be both an informative text and an experiential guide, it is highly recommended that you engage in all of the in-chapter prompts and exercises, so that you not only cognitively understand the concepts, but also integrate them at both an emotional and physiological level.

Throughout the book, you will find **Practice & Reflection** boxes that offer opportunities for experiential exercises and reflection. These are highly valuable invitations to pause, reflect on, and integrate the concepts introduced throughout the chapter. Doing so will exponentially increase the impact of exploring this workbook.

For all exercises or prompts that invite written reflections or journal entries, it is recommended that you choose a special journal devoted solely to accompany this workbook, so that you can keep all of your thoughts and reflections on this journey in one sacred place. For consistency, it is best to have one place to go for the writing practices and reflection questions posed throughout the workbook. Consistency is a critical key to progress, especially when it comes to internally transformative practices like the ones you will find in the following pages.

As you begin this journey, it is also extremely important to keep in mind that only you know what is best for you. If any prompts you encounter feel too overwhelming in the moment, pause and ask yourself if you might need to take a break and complete them when you are feeling more centered. If certain things you read in the pages to come do not feel helpful or right for you, leave them out and proceed with the tools and concepts that do. And most importantly, be vigilant with your own self-care; make sure that before delving deeply into this work, you have identified an accessible support network readily available to you, one that includes both personal and professional relationships you can rely on if at any time something surfaces that feels too big to navigate on your own. This work should not be a crusade characterized by even more self-criticism and a falsely perceived need to do or be more than you already are; by its very nature, this work asks you to meet yourself exactly *where* you are, and to come to the meeting with slowness, gentleness, a willingness to listen to your own needs, and an unprecedented amount of self-compassion.

In the next few pages is an introductory **Practice & Reflection** box to help get you started. Don't worry if some things don't come naturally quite yet. The pages ahead will guide you further on this transformative journey.

BOX:
PRACTICE & REFLECTION

Getting Started

To prepare ourselves for the journey ahead, there are a few things we can practice to start to build our muscles for the exercise of just *being* with our own emotions, and committing to embrace them exactly as they are.

On the next few pages is one *action*, one set of *reflection* questions, and one introductory *meditation* to get us started.

ACTION:

Making sacred space

It is important, just as with any new practice, that we make time for leaning into our feelings. Because it is such a new and often delicate process, with this practice in particular, it is best to carve out both time and physical space that will really allow you to honor your emotions in a peaceful, interruption-free environment.

Whether it's during your morning coffee, some other regularly occurring period of solitude, or a new time you create for yourself, doing this will allow you to become acquainted with the very process of feeling your feelings.

Creating a sacred space is simply about acknowledging that you are making room for a ritual that means something to you. It is about truly honoring your relationship to yourself and your commitment to growth. In that light, creating a sacred space is less about what or where the actual space is, and more about your intention and level of self-compassion in creating it.

Reflection:

What has brought you here?

The questions below are a guide to help you move into the practice of becoming more aware of your emotions and your relationship to your emotions. There are no right or wrong answers; it is simply an exercise in awareness-building and reflection:

- What has drawn you to pick up this book? Why are you here, at this particular moment on your path, reading about these concepts, and what is your intention for yourself in working with this book?

- Do you also have an intention for your wider community, or the world, as you explore these concepts? If so, what is it?

- How would you describe your current relationship with your own feelings? To help you answer this question, you might try to imagine your feelings as another entity or being, and then describe the way that you treat or relate to it. Do you, for example, ignore, judge, or fear your emotions? Do you pretend not to notice them, or keep yourself going at such a strong momentum that you don't make space for them? Do your emotions confuse you? Do they amaze you or leave you in awe? Do you find your emotions beautiful? Do you offer them love and space to just exist? As you can start to see, there are many different ways that we can be in relationship with our emotions.

MEDITATION:

Trusting Your Own Present Moment Experience

*Note: for all of the meditations in this workbook, it is recommended that you first briefly read through the guided instructions, doing your best to absorb the general flow of the exercise, and then go fully into your own meditative space without looking back at the text too often (unless you need to remind yourself of a certain part of the practice). Doing it this way will help you stay more present to the experience rather than overly engaged with the words on the page; it will allow your mind and body to relax more fully, and therefore to more completely receive the potential benefits of these exercises.

To prepare yourself for this short introductory meditation, find a comfortable position, either seated or lying down, and either close your eyes or keep them gently open.

Taking deep breaths in through the nose and out through the mouth, lightly bring attention to your senses.

Allow the awareness of your senses to increase while you practice fully *receiving* what you feel:

- Allow your ears to open and just listen. Listen like you would for a train while on the platform. Stay open and curious. *Fully receive each sound.*

- Allow your nose to open in the same way. *Fully receive each smell.*

- Now move your tongue around your mouth and notice the taste. *Fully receive each taste.*

- Become aware how the textures of your clothing feel on your skin. Relax the body enough to actually *fully receive each sensation of touch.*

- As you notice your experiences, practice doing just that: noticing and receiving. Without judgment, assessment, labeling, or thinking about anything at all, allow yourself to become aware of what is happening for you in each moment.

If you would like, take a moment to write down some thoughts about your experience.

Susan Kullman

Susan Kullman

CHAPTER ONE

LEARNING A NEW LANGUAGE OF EMOTION

"This place where you are right now,
God circled on a map for you."

- HAFIZ

Susan Kullman

THERE IS AN IMPORTANT PARADIGM shift currently unfolding at this point on the trajectory of human evolution—a shift that pertains to new ways of experiencing and reframing our relationship to ourselves and our emotions. Therefore, the concepts and practices discussed in this book constitute, in a sense, an utterly new language, one that could not have entered into the mainstream collective discourse before now because it has, in part, been born of relatively recent advancements in behavioral sciences and wellness fields such as neuroscience, psychology, and biomechanics, to name a few.

Because the concept of cultivating a new relationship to our own emotions is still in its infancy, learning this new language, just like the process for learning any new language, takes time, patience, and self-compassion. And, as with any new language, in order to create a platform for fluency, it is best to begin with the basics.

One of the most important fundamentals of enhancing our relationship to our emotions is to strengthen our ability to embrace that which feels uncomfortable, rather than to run from it.

The famous poet, Hafiz, states in the quote above, "This place where you are right now/ God circled on a map for you." Spiritual beliefs aside, the all-inclusive truth of this line is that no matter what any of us may experience in a given moment, no matter how chaotic or upsetting things may feel, there is always something significant about what arises within us in any given moment, and what arises always offers a key to our own growth and healing.

To keep this in mind as we are experiencing our emotions is to take the first critical step towards learning this new language, and towards re-navigating an entirely new relationship with ourselves. That first critical step is what we can call *emotional awareness*.

When we allow ourselves to move through every aspect of our experiences with nonjudgmental *awareness* of what we feel—resisting the reactive urge to avoid, push away, or run from the darker places on our personal maps, and embracing equally the beautiful, the uncomfortable, and even, at times, the seemingly unbearable—the learnings offered by these experiences become much more accessible to us. Given this new space to *just be*, our most uncomfortable emotions may sometimes even become lanterns that transform the darkness, providing greater clarity and lighting our way forward.

Furthermore, when we begin to view our emotions through the more objective lens of awareness without judgment, this change in relationship to our emotions allows us to respond to them in new ways that help us transcend former barriers to growth and transformation.

Yet how can we begin to heighten our emotional awareness, thereby making space for *all* of our emotions to exist so that we can harness them for our personal growth, when for so long we have entrained ourselves—psychologically, intellectually, and even physically—to ignore and deeply bury that which does not feel "good"?

How do we retrain ourselves to relax our fears when it comes to simply feeling our feelings?

The answer is this: practice.

We must practice—with patience, consistency, and self-compassion—getting to know ourselves more deeply. Being with ourselves and all of our emotions. Committing to what is.

There are many ways that we can engage in this practice, yet importantly, they all require quiet time for self-connection and self-reflection. Just as in our relationships with others, in order to get to know ourselves more authentically and to trust ourselves more completely, we must devote time to truly being with ourselves.

Many of us may have a hard time with stillness because when things around us become quiet, we sometimes notice a marked increase in our "mind chatter," perhaps the feeling of bouncing around from thought to thought, or potentially even a heightened sense of physical pain or discomfort. These sensations might feel fine for some, and either mildly or extremely uncomfortable for others. Everyone is different.

In the face of challenges with stillness, one thing we can do to help ourselves is to awaken a deeper awareness of our own physical body, as this offers an avenue to begin trusting the safety of our internal processes. The process of becoming more aware of the physical body is called *interoception*, a term that refers specifically to the perception of sensations from inside the body, and even includes the perception of physical sensations related to things like internal organ function, such as heartbeat, respiration, satiety, and autonomic nervous system activity.

All of these functions of the physical body are related to our emotions, and increasing awareness of them can help us to deepen our trust in ourselves, in our emotions, and in the stillness we need to cultivate a stronger relationship with all of these things. Practicing this process of interoception is a crucial step in learning how to simply *be* with ourselves in the present moment, and to know all aspects of our own experience.

Forging a deeper relationship with the physical body is a critical aspect of deepening our emotional awareness, so that we can cultivate the ability to fully *experience* what we feel rather than judge or avoid it. The recognition that fully experiencing our emotions is in part a *somatic* practice, meaning it also takes place at the level of the physical body rather than solely in the mind, is paramount to becoming more open to everything we feel. Experiencing our emotions, including how they feel in the physical body, even activates a different part of the brain than simply thinking about them.

Later in this book, we will more deeply explore the somatic impact of emotions, but for now it is important simply to understand that being in a new relationship with our feelings requires that we not only release intellectual judgment of our emotions, but also that we allow ourselves to relax into the physical sensations that arise in the body whenever we feel any emotion at all. The body is a beautiful practice ground and learning tool that is always available to us; we can harness its intelligence to cultivate trust in the stillness we need for self-reflection and self-connection, and to learn how to experience our emotions in a much deeper way.

It is important to highlight that this re-navigation of our relationship to our own emotions, both intellectually and somatically, is an introspective process that is intended to be privately engaged *with* ourselves and *for* ourselves—cultivating this new relationship is for the purpose of, first and foremost, developing greater confidence, security, and comfort within.

BOX: PRACTICE AND REFLECTION

Building Emotional Awareness and Getting Comfortable with our Feelings

Through Meditation

The seed of self-transformation begins in stillness. In order to develop a stronger, more authentic relationship with our own emotions, which requires that we relax into what we are actually feeling, we must first and foremost practice being in this stillness

Getting comfortable with ourselves begins with gently being with ourselves, just as we would sit with a best friend.

Using this fundamental exercise, make a commitment to spend a few minutes every day building your relationship with yourself in this way:

As you sit, take a few gentle breaths and allow your body to gradually come into stillness.

Begin again, as we did in the first meditation, to fully experience your external environment through your senses:

- Open your ears. Notice what you hear if you just listen.

- Open your nose. Notice what you smell if you just smell.

- Notice the temperature in the room. Allow yourself to just relax your body and receive the temperature.

- Notice the way some of the fabrics you are wearing might feel against your skin.

Next, begin to experience your internal environment through the physical sensations of the body:

- Begin by relaxing your muscles, and try even to visualize relaxing every single component of your body —all the organs, sinews, and soft tissue that keep you alive. This may feel unusual at first, but practicing it can deepen your ability to truly relax.

- Sense how the fabric of the skin begins to loosen and organize itself.

- What shifts do you sense in your heart rate?

- What shifts do you sense in your respiration?

- Continue to become aware of and curious about how you hold or tighten certain areas of the body.

- What happens when you bring simple awareness to these holding patterns?

Allow yourself to sit and gently observe these experiences, and simply welcome each moment as it comes. At the conclusion of this exercise, write down some reflections or insights.

Through Writing

Writing can be an incredibly powerful and transformative tool that can also help us get to know ourselves and our emotions a little bit more, and to become more comfortable with being present to them.

This simple writing exercise is most effective as a *daily* practice—it is important to engage with this exercise to some extent each day in order to begin to cultivate a new relationship with emotion. Just like any good relationship, evolving it takes time and dedication.

Every day, at least once—starting in this moment now—write a journal entry that begins with the words:

Today I feel...

Allow whatever comes to mind to spill out onto the page. Do not edit your thoughts. Write as if no one is watching you or reading what you write—not even you!

Although this may sound over-simplified, becoming present to our emotions without censoring them is a critical step in beginning to build emotional awareness.

As you write down your feelings, try to also become aware of what arises in terms of your bodily sensations. Do you feel a shift in body temperature? A building tension in a particular area of your body? A tingling sensation in your arms? If so, write these down as well.

Also, try to focus on the adjectives or phrases that describe *how* you are feeling rather than actually labeling the emotions themselves.

For example: tingling in the chest, heavy in the heart, a lump in the stomach, etc.

This practice will help you reduce the common tendency to try to cerebrally process or analyze your feelings, and will instead connect you to them as the natural, organic experiences that they are.

THE EGO AND THE WITNESS:
LETTING YOUR GUARD DOWN

When it comes to our relationship with our emotions, moving from judgment, avoidance, and fear, to awareness, allowing, and experiencing may seem easier said than done. Yet in addition to cultivating quiet self-connection and physiological awareness, there are also some important concepts that we can integrate to make this shift feel less daunting, and realistically attainable.

One of the fundamental building blocks that we must secure in order to construct a relationship with emotion that is rooted in awareness and allowing, and thus to let down common defenses to fully experiencing our feelings, is to learn to distinguish between two very different and equally important parts of ourselves. We will call these two parts *the ego* and *the witness.*

In order to understand this important distinction, it is helpful first to outline what we mean when we use these terms.

The ego, as defined in this workbook, refers to the part of us that, since birth, has had the singular goal of protecting us and keeping us alive. It is the part of our psyches that houses mechanisms geared toward physical and emotional survival, and that orients us to the practical realities of the physical world—such as time, money, societal standards and protocol, the physical body, and so on. We can see, therefore, that the role of the ego is extremely important, and that we need it, to a certain extent, in order to live functional lives.

It is only when the ego bypasses the healthy boundaries of its purposeful role—for example, when it persists in using old modes of self-protection that no longer serve us—that we might begin to experience certain pathologies characteristic of the ego. The same is true of anything, however; what is helpful in moderation can quickly become unhealthy in excess.

We will never, in this work, seek to demonize the ego. This is not only because doing so is an affront to the ways in which it does truly serve us, but also because, as with our emotions, what we try to push away will inevitably become stronger. It is therefore somewhat of a self-fulfilling prophecy to attempt to suppress the ego and label it as "bad," for in the act of denying this part of ourselves, we may actually unintentionally drive it into unhealthy territory.

An ideal way to be with the ego, instead, is to offer gratitude for the role it plays in keeping us well, and simultaneously to recognize when we might need a different part of ourselves to come to the forefront in order to make progress in certain areas of our lives, such as in the realms of emotional growth and awareness.

The witness is the part of ourselves whose strength is to aid us in becoming more vulnerable with our own emotions and in feeling safe to fully experience them.

The witness is so-called because we can think of it as the part of ourselves that "simply watches". We can say that it is "awareness itself". The witness is not located in a specific place in the body, nor is it characterized by one particular feeling, but rather it is the part of us that *notices* our physical and emotional feelings, and is able to respond with self-compassion and calm, rather than self-judgment or fear.

The amazing thing is that, with practice, we can actually train ourselves to become *aware* of this state of *awareness*.

The benefit in doing so is that the more attuned to this state of awareness we become, the more easily we can deliberately call to the forefront the witness within when we want to feel safer leaning into our uncomfortable emotions. The witness can also help us move forward when we want to do anything that scares us.

The reason that harnessing the witness is so helpful when we desire to move beyond fear is that, when we assume this inner position, we become neutral and nonreactive observers of our own experiences. This does *not* mean that we detach from our experiences—on the contrary, to be in a true state of healthy witnessing entails deep presence and connection to whatever is happening in the mind and body. The key is that when we harness the witness, we are not judging or reacting to these experiences, but rather, simply noticing them with presence and self-compassion.

Let's look at this through the lens of a physical example. This can apply to any physical sensation in the body, but for now let's imagine how some of us might typically respond to the very slight beginning of a headache.

For many of us, when we feel this kind of sensation arise, even though the feeling itself might be quite subtle at first, our minds can often instigate a flood of secondary, fear-based, and neurophysiologically habituated responses. These responses might take the form of thoughts such as "Oh no, I feel a headache coming on and now my day is going to be ruined," or "Now I'm never going to be able to accomplish that task I was supposed to do later today," or "Why do I have a headache? What if there's something really wrong with me?", or a plethora of other ways we sometimes respond when an uncomfortable sensation arises in the body.

When these reactive thought cycles (which are characteristic of the ego) begin, they themselves release a cascade of fear-related neurochemicals that put an even greater burden on the physical body. Thus, by reacting to the initial feeling of a small headache, we have now added secondary layers of judgment, reactivity, and fear to our otherwise potentially isolated experience. This reactive thought process can of course then elevate the headache even further, eventually fulfilling that original fear.

However, if we switch into the mode of the witness as soon as we notice a headache beginning, we might instead generate thoughts such as, "I notice that I have the feeling of a slight headache," or even "Oh, isn't that interesting?" And for the witness, such observations are conclusive. Rather than enter into an ensuing inner dialogue of drama, chaos, confusion, or fear (which is where the ego mind so often beckons us), the witness simply observes, welcoming any experience exactly as it is, with objective statements of observation and curiosity in place of heightened reactivity.

When we harness the witness within, we allow experiences to pass through our consciousness without judging or overidentifying with them. We become neutral in our response without disconnecting from it, and achieve a state of gentle and simple awareness. This also allows us to more clearly distinguish when we might need to take action to help ourselves, when we need to offer ourselves something internally such as greater self-compassion, or when we need simply to sit quietly, breathe, and rest the mind and body.

In contrast to the flood of fear-based thoughts that the ego mind, well-meaning yet misguided, often unleashes in the face of uncomfortable physical sensations, taking the inner position of the witness not only prevents those secondary layers of fear and their resulting cyclical impact on the body, it also actively creates an inner environment of safety, security, and calm—similar to when a stable parent, partner, or friend supports us to return from inner turmoil to a place of peace.

In this case, though, we instead learn to create this safe and stable space for ourselves. And when we do this, it generates a drastically different cascade of neurochemicals, ones that help us continue to feel better, both emotionally *and* physically.

While the example above refers to physical experience, we can also apply identical practice to moments when we notice uncomfortable emotions or thoughts arising within.

If we simply notice these emotions and thoughts with presence, self-compassion and curiosity, we create an internal environment of safety and security for our emotions to move through us without fearing that experience.

To do so, we can remind ourselves that while we are *having* the experience of these emotions, they are not *who we are*. In fact, we can start to see this even more clearly as we practice harnessing the witness, for by definition, if we are able to notice something, such as our emotions, doesn't it make sense that we cannot simultaneously *be* the very thing that we are witnessing?

There must be a part of us that is more than *just* that thing we are witnessing, a part of us that is *doing* the witnessing. We will work more with this idea in the **Practice & Reflection** box at the end of this section.

Again, it is important to note that we never want to mistake witnessing for detachment. Detachment is yet another defense mechanism that arises when we *do not* feel safe, and therefore shut down to our experiences and feelings. Witnessing involves the opposite—to create a landscape of inner safety and security that allows us to *more fully* experience our emotions as the deeply feeling human beings that we are. The ultimate benefit of harnessing the witness is that it helps us to become *more* present to and connected with our emotions by creating a safer environment in which to experience them.

Also important to note is that the ego and the witness are not the only two parts of our consciousness. Each of us is a highly complex being, with multiple "parts" or levels of consciousness that, ideally, work in unison to ensure our wellbeing. When an imbalance arises regarding the roles that each of these parts inhabit, we experience the impacts of that imbalance, either emotionally or physically. When we can bring those parts of ourselves back into coordination with one another so that they serve us according to their respective strengths, we regain a sense of stability and wellbeing.

While they are not the only two parts, the ego and the witness are two *primary* aspects of consciousness that, when out of balance with one another, or when harnessed for the wrong purpose, can really impact our ability to be in "right relationship" with our emotions. Therefore, to create the level of awareness we need in order to fully experience our emotions, we must first become acquainted with the particular strengths and weaknesses of both the ego and the witness, so that we know the most aligned purposes each one serves.

It is essential that we understand which one is best to summon for support when we want to travel to deeper places within ourselves or to dismantle outdated defense mechanisms that we no longer need to protect us (i.e., the witness), and which one to call on when we need to navigate urgent situations, or to help establish financial or structural security for ourselves (i.e, the ego).

As we can see from these examples alone, both the ego and the witness are extremely valuable, and even indispensable. However, it is vital that we learn when to harness each one. For while both the ego and the witness are integral to our existence, they possess vastly different characteristics, strengths and weaknesses.

Just like it is helpful to know which tool in a toolbox will accomplish a particular task most efficiently, it is critical to our self-growth that we learn which situations and goals call for each of these different aspects of self.

While the ego serves some extremely important functions in our lives, it is simply not the correct tool to use to accomplish particular goals. We learned earlier that the ego has the tendency sometimes to create mechanisms for self-defense and self-protection that outlast their usefulness, and when this happens—when we are operating with old, outdated software as our primary means for survival—the very mechanisms that at one time may have kept us safe can actually begin to hinder us, or even harm us, in the present.

This, in turn, can ironically lead to us feeling less safety rather than more. In order to upgrade our systems to be able to generate a true sense of safety and belonging in the world, we need to first identify that there is an outdated system running somewhere within us.

This is often a very difficult task. It can be extremely challenging to know when we are using these old forms of self-protection, since they have likely been ingrained in our psyches since childhood, or even birth.

For example, many of us run an old operating system that tells us that to be emotionally vulnerable is unsafe, and therefore, in order to protect us, the ego may help us to build walls around our emotions and around the parts of us that would otherwise seek to experience and move through our emotions.

Perhaps at one time in our lives this kind of protection was helpful and even necessary—when we were children with a lesser sense of safety, choice, and boundaries, as well as less developed emotional and cognitive skills to support us in navigating these inner experiences. As adults, however, many of us now have much greater access to appropriate levels of understanding and self-empowerment to make it okay, and even beneficial, for us to feel what we feel completely. But because we are still operating based on our old protective systems, we often unconsciously default to shutting down our emotions and building walls within.

The problem with defaulting to old protective mechanisms that developed during childhood is that, as adults, it is actually often *more* beneficial and serving to our growth and transformation to become more vulnerable with ourselves, to release our old defense mechanisms, and to fully experience our emotions.

It is only when we realize that we need to pull a different tool from our emotional toolboxes—becoming comfortable with our own emotional vulnerability, in this case—that we can successfully interrupt old cycles, and learn new ways of helping ourselves feel safe, healthy, and balanced.

To convince ourselves that a new way of being is safe, however, is not always an easy task; it is essentially rewiring old neural pathways to create a new "normal" for the entire nervous system. That is why it requires great consistency, and deeply self-compassionate practice.

And the part of ourselves we need to call on to help enhance our levels of self-compassion, self-awareness, and comfort with emotional vulnerability, is *not* the ego. It is the witness.

ॐ

BOX: PRACTICE & REFLECTION

Practicing Calling Forth the Inner Witness

To practice calling forth and strengthening your inner witness, try the following exercise:

Gently close your eyes and bring to mind a series of simple images: a car, a school, a boat, a house, a grassy field, an ocean, a dog, a child, a table, a chair, etc.

Continue to cycle through these simple images in your mind.

Once you have done this a few times, reflect on the experience you just had, and ask yourself: *Who is it who was thinking of those images?*

Of course, it was you who was thinking of them. But what part of you was it? When we use simple images like this, it is easy to see that we are not completely synonymous with these things, although we are thinking *about* them. We are *thinking of* a school, a house, a car, etc., but we *are not* a school, a house, or a car.

The same is true of any thought or emotion that we may experience.

Now try the same thing with any emotions or sensations you might be feeling at this moment. Allow yourself to feel your emotions and sensations completely, while also remembering, just like with the simple images we just brought to mind, that you are not entirely your emotions or sensations—there is a part of you that is *observing* or having the experience of the emotion or sensation, and therefore, it cannot be true that you *are* that emotion or sensation itself.

You might want to pause here and ask yourself the following question:

If I am aware of the sensations running through my body when I experience an emotion, what part of me is it that has this awareness in the first place?

Write down any thoughts, insights, or questions that arise during or after this exercise.

FOUR GUIDING PRINCIPLES
ABOUT FEELINGS

Using the witness within to observe and experience emotions from an objective perspective can help diminish the lofty power our emotions may appear to wield over us, and can re-empower us to fully feel them, and thus to navigate them with greater ease and dynamism.

To begin to retrain our perceptions of and responses to feeling, one important thing we can do is to explore four *primary* objective principles about what emotions really are. Integrating these clear concepts will broaden and shift our emotional lexicon, thus helping us to cultivate this new relationship to emotion—one in which we *allow*, rather than brace against, what we feel.

Let it be noted that there is an extremely important distinction between feeling our feelings and thinking about our feelings. Integrating the guiding principles below will help us understand and practice experiencing this important difference, and will help us gain enough perspective to begin to distinguish between the stories behind our emotions and the emotions themselves. In doing so, we can retrain our old habit of conflating these two experiences and lean into a now wider space for exploring our relationship to our thoughts and feelings.

Before we even begin to explore these principles, though, we must first establish one that is most fundamental, and upon which all the others rest.

It is simply this: we *all* have feelings, and we are all experiencing some kind of feeling most of the time.

As human beings, every one of us has emotions that are both comfortable and uncomfortable, light and dark, easy and challenging. We are electrical and energetic beings who experience emotions based on our perceptions and beliefs, and we are also easily affected by external sources such as other human beings, animals, nature, technology, and anything else in our environments. There is always energy flowing through our bodies, contributing to our present-moment experience. Whether we realize it or not, we are always feeling *something*.

Often, we lose awareness of our sensations and feelings, primarily because we are more involved with and aware of the thoughts in our minds than the energy coursing through our bodies. Sometimes our mental chatter can be so seductive, entertaining, and consuming that we might unintentionally and unknowingly disconnect from our bodies, meaning that we turn off or shut ourselves down to recognizing the organic signals of even our most basic human needs. This shows up in the form of moments when we might find ourselves so involved in our tasks or thoughts that we forget to eat, rest, or even go to the bathroom, or that we fail to notice how tired we truly are until we stop moving.

The four guiding principles about feelings presented here aim to provide the foundations for a paradigm shift away from our culturally revered and encouraged tendency to **understand**, **analyze** and **intellectualize** our emotions —and a movement instead towards **embracing** and **relaxing** into them. Many of us may have heard this suggestion before, though we may not have really understood how to accomplish this, or what it really feels like.

Just like with any new skill set we learn, when it comes to our emotions, we have to first integrate a new group of basic foundations or rules of thumb. This integration provides a solid platform for growth and practice that can help stabilize the uncertainty that often accompanies navigating new skills at more advanced stages in the learning process.

Here are the four primary guiding principles for objectively understanding our feelings:

1. Feelings are visceral experiences, and what we don't allow ourselves to feel stays with us.

Counter to the way we typically talk and think about feelings in our culture, they are, in large part, physiological sensations in the body. Though our feelings are of course also intricately connected to our minds and thoughts, they are part of a grand network of neurochemicals, cells, organs, and glands. They are visceral experiences, each with different accompanying sensations. When we begin to reflect on and experience our feelings in this light, we may find that we can gain the degree of objectivity we need in order to lessen self-judgment.

Most of us often tend to over-identify with our feelings, as if we *are* the feelings themselves; if we feel angry, for example, we may interpret it to mean something negative about ourselves. This way of thinking about our feelings usually leads to a perceived need to defend our own emotions, whether to ourselves or to others. This defense then actually prevents us from truly feeling what we feel, as it redirects our energy and attention towards heightening the defense and away from truly experiencing the feeling itself.

It is much healthier for us to fully feel our emotions for a short time (sometimes even ten to fifteen minutes can be sufficient) than to keep them blocked and thereby allow them to occupy space in the body and mind. Blocked or suppressed emotions often cause physical symptoms such as muscle tension, dysfunctional movement patterns, inflammation, as well as an internal resistance to shifts in perception—even when those shifts would likely generate greater health, happiness, mental stability, and longevity.

When we continue to carry our unprocessed emotions in body and mind, it often causes us to unconsciously react to situations in a way that only generates more of the challenging thing to which we are reacting. This is the pattern that underlies a very human tendency to sometimes persist in creating that which we do not want; our blocked emotions contaminate all the ways we approach life.

While it is common to believe that allowing ourselves to feel uncomfortable emotions is too painful or too much to handle, it is typically *not the feeling itself* that is uncomfortable; rather, it is the *resistance* to the feeling that is in fact an even bigger source of discomfort. Therefore, to truly give ourselves permission to embrace our emotions, and to allow their accompanying visceral sensations to completely move through us, is to free ourselves from the uncomfortable hold of those emotions and any blocks they may create to fulfilling our true potential.

When we view our feelings simply as visceral experiences, we can create the distance from them that we need in order to allow ourselves to fully feel them and their accompanying physical sensations without shame or judgment.

Remember: we *have* feelings, but we are *not* our feelings.

BOX: PRACTICE & REFLECTION PRINCIPLE #1

Feelings are Visceral Experiences

Every emotion gives rise to different visceral sensations, and those sensations also vary from person to person, though there is often overlap in our individual experiences.

Anxiety, for example, might feel jittery, while sadness might feel heavy.

Using as many adjectives as possible, write a brief description about your visceral experience of each of the following emotions:

Fear	Sadness	Anger
Sorrow	Frustration	Disappointment
Envy	Worry	Hurt
Anxiety	Shame	Embarrassment

Next, you can also try this exercise:

Call to mind a certain situation in your life that caused you to feel what you consider to be a negative or uncomfortable emotion. Become aware of how thinking of that event affects your internal environment—what type of sensations arise in your body?

Resist the urge to label these sensations as any particular emotion. Instead, simply describe them using adjectives.

- Do they have certain textures or temperatures?

- Where are they located in your body?

- Can you even describe them in color?

While you may experience thoughts or dialogue in your mind about the particular situation that generated these sensations, do your best to allow the visceral to be your primary experience in this moment.

As you relax your body, stay aware of the sensations that arise, allow yourself to be curious about them, and *allow them to be ok.*

While it may not feel comfortable at first, gently remind yourself that there is absolutely nothing wrong with these sensations; they are all natural.

Consider, even, that experiencing them may be exactly right for you at this moment.

As your body relaxes into these sensations, do your best to stay with them until you feel that they have "integrated". To feel integration is to feel a sense of completion or neutralization, and this feels different for everyone.

One way to know when your body has completed the degree of integration it needs in this moment is when you sense a softening of the naturally occurring resistance to actually doing the exercise itself. Other times, you may simply sense that you feel complete for now, and possibly even more relaxed and open than when you began.

Please note that it may take multiple attempts to experience a softening of resistance, or to know what completion or integration feels like for you; this does not mean that you are not "getting it". Every time we engage in this kind of practice of fully experiencing our emotions without judgment, we are retraining our nervous systems to this positive habit. And rewiring the nervous system, of course, takes both time and practice.

2. Feeling and thinking are mutually exclusive.

It is not possible to think your feelings. This may sound obvious, but it is actually quite often that we confuse thinking and feeling. We may believe we are *experiencing* an emotion when in fact we are merely *thinking* about that emotion. Although thought does share an important relationship with emotion, it is an entirely separate function that occupies and arises from a distinct part of the brain.

When we use reasoning to try to understand a particular aspect—or multiple aspects—of a situation, to figure out a solution to a perceived problem, or to reflect *about* an emotion, we are in a state of thinking rather than feeling.

This is a very important distinction. If we confuse thinking and feeling, we will likely be unable to recognize when we are suppressing our emotions and may wrongly assume that because we are thinking about a certain situation, we are actually experiencing our feelings about it.

In fact, though, we are usually doing just the opposite. For when we engage the thinking mind, we typically *suppress* our emotions. This is another example of a well intentioned yet misguided protective mechanism that our unconscious minds use to try to keep us safe, but that often ends up impeding our healing and transformation.

In order to fully experience our emotions—allowing them to more readily dissipate, and thus to return us to a state of balance that propels healthy action and growth—we must learn to recognize this distinction between thinking and feeling. Furthermore, we must learn to recognize how these two states feel differently in our minds and bodies.

This, of course, can be challenging for everyone, since the human brain is constantly thinking, solving, assessing, and reasoning. Meditation and mindfulness practice therefore serve as helpful tools for forming a deeper relationship with our emotions.

Susan Kullman

BOX: PRACTICE & REFLECTION PRINCIPLE #2

Feeling and Thinking are Mutually Exclusive

Bring to mind a situation that creates an uncomfortable emotion, and try to identify the distinction between the visceral feeling (the descriptive adjectives you wrote down in the Practice and Reflection box for *Principle #1*), and the story that gives rise to those feelings.

To do this, begin by simply thinking about the story as you typically would, and notice how this feels in your mind and body. Write down some adjectives to describe how it feels.

Now pause and ask yourself the following question:

If there is nothing to think about or figure out right now, what is there?

Allow yourself just to become aware of the feelings in your body, and practice simply witnessing them—as if you were observing them compassionately from a distance.

Then, allow yourself to fully receive them, to relax into their vibration rather than brace against them.

Importantly, try to experience the feelings themselves rather than to think anything about them.

Now notice how *this* feels in your mind and body, and write down some adjectives to describe the experience.

Finally, take some time to reflect on whether or not there was a difference between these two states of mind and body—between thinking about the story behind the feeling and experiencing the feeling itself. If there was, what would you say was the difference?

Please note that learning to distinguish between feeling our feelings and thinking about the stories behind our feelings not only takes practice, but it also truly takes trust. It takes trust that we can in fact release our strong grip on attention to thoughts, and instead allow the vibrations of our feelings themselves to run their course.

When we first start this process, our attention will often oscillate microsecond-by-microsecond between feeling and thought. The key in this practice is to cultivate the skill of focusing solely on our feelings for increasingly longer durations of time, with an awareness that is gentle and relaxed, rather than overly intense or effortful.

Again, this takes practice, so make sure to be patient with yourself!

3. Feelings are always valid—they are never right, wrong, good or bad.

When you feel an emotion, what matters most—and what is always true—is that you are *in fact* experiencing it. In other words, whether a feeling you experience is a reflection of what is actually happening in the present moment or is a projection that arises from neurological conditioning due to past experiences, it remains true that you *are* nonetheless experiencing that emotion, and that experience is very real.

We often fall into the trap of labeling our emotions as good or bad, right or wrong, logical or illogical, valid or not. However, if we wish to experience, process, and move through life with a degree of authenticity and inner peace, we cannot subject our emotions to this kind of categorization.

Labeling and judging our emotions diminishes peace and balance because it heightens our reactivity. The moment we judge an emotion as good or bad, right or wrong, we instantly create within ourselves a reaction to that judgment.

Judgment yields reactivity, and reactivity is a state of the mind and nervous system that then leads to thoughts, words, actions, and often other secondary feelings that arise instantly, like a knee-jerk reflex. In this state, there is little time and space for present moment awareness, and it can often catapult us into unhealthy spirals of thought and action.

Often, we may not realize when we are labeling an emotion, because it is a habit that for most of us has become deeply ingrained. It takes a very conscious practice to retrain ourselves, in the moment of experiencing any feeling, to allow it just to be present without self-judgment.

In order to begin to change our relationship to our emotions, we must learn to validate that each one, regardless of where it comes from, is real. For, of course, we can only form an authentic relationship with something when we first acknowledge that it exists.

It is important to clarify here the distinction between accepting a feeling as real and acting based upon that feeling. While every emotion we experience is real, knowing the difference between one that justifies an actual present moment response and one that is a reaction to our pre-conditioning and past experience is extremely important.

For example, we may feel the justified urge to defend ourselves in a situation where our physical safety is truly being threatened, and rightfully act on this feeling. Yet, in another situation, we might become enraged by certain words casually uttered by a friend because it unconsciously reminds us of a past experience and feeling. In cases like the latter, it helps to be able to pause before acting on our feelings so that we know what actions are appropriate and healthy.

However, no matter what, we always want to validate that the emotion we are experiencing is real, so that we do not minimize, analyze, or ignore it. It is actually this process of validating ourselves that helps us learn to distinguish which situations call for immediate action, which ones call for reflection before acting, and which ones call solely for self-reflection and self-compassion without action.

Let it also be clarified that it is not only situations posing threat to our physical safety that justify action; even subtly abusive or harmful situations in the realm of verbal and emotional interaction can absolutely also warrant strong action in order to take care of ourselves. Again, though, the best way to gain clarity on whether or not to act on our emotions is first to validate them to ourselves. The moment we accept an emotion as real, we take the initial step towards knowing how to navigate it, how to navigate the situation that gave rise to it, and eventually, how to move beyond it.

When we simply allow our emotions to be as they are without assessing them, we create in the mind and nervous system a space for stillness. This increases our time for reflection, which then yields much healthier and more productive states of emotional awareness and emotional response.

BOX: PRACTICE & REFLECTION PRINCIPLE #3

Feelings are Always Valid— They are Never Right. Wrong. Good or Bad

Write down your answers to the following questions as you reflect on them:

Bring to mind a situation that has posed some level of conflict for you. Is there a part of you that feels defensive about this situation, even to yourself?

When you think about this situation, do you notice your mind noisily "chattering" or repeatedly analyzing whether or not you have a *right* to feel what you are feeling?

Have you ever caught yourself telling the story about this situation to someone else, hoping that their reaction confirms your right to feel the way you do?

These common responses to inner conflict are all signals that you are likely judging your own feelings. Yet when you want to truly feel your feelings, it is paramount to allow yourself to experience them without judgment and without the attempt to "figure them out" or justify them.

Try offering yourself some nonjudgmental compassion for your feelings about this situation, and notice if that changes the way the situation or story feels in your body.

One way to do this is to engage in compassionate dialogue with yourself. For example, you can say to yourself some of the following kind and supportive things:

- It is normal that I feel hurt or sad at this moment.

- I give myself permission to feel exactly the way that I feel at this moment.

- There is nothing I need to figure out right now—I am allowed to feel what I feel.

- If I knew that it was very safe to feel my feelings right now, I would...

- Even though I cannot figure this out right now, I feel ...

Now you can write down how it felt to offer yourself this kind of nonjudgmental compassion, and simply to have experienced your emotions.

What other kind, supportive, and compassionate things might you say to yourself to let yourself know that it is ok and safe to feel your feelings?

One way to come up with these kinds of phrases for healthy and compassionate inner dialogue is to think of what you might say to someone you deeply care about. Sometimes it is easier for us to think of what we might say to others from a place of compassion, but it is paramount that we also learn to apply that same compassion and support to ourselves first and foremost.

4. Feelings are NOT always rational—they are habitual records of the past.

Our emotions *do not have to make sense*—to us, or to others—and in fact, very often, they do not. While, as the last principle explored, all of our feelings are always *valid*, this does not mean that they are always *justified*. That is, while all feelings are very real experiences, they may not always correlate directly to what is truly happening in the present moment. This is because our emotions are: 1) habitual; and 2) records of the past.

Neurophysiologically speaking, humans can in fact develop addiction to particular emotions in much the same way that we develop addiction to substances or activities. As with all addiction, our attachment to particular emotions and our resulting tendency to experience them repeatedly throughout our lives comes about via habit and neurochemical conditioning. Through this conditioning, we "practice" certain feelings over and over again at the cellular level until they become habit for our nervous systems. This process then has the potential to create a default inner state of being that eventually comes to feel "like ourselves".

Of course, we may sometimes shift out of this state, but because the nervous system has been conditioned to experience it, we will almost always eventually unconsciously create or react to a situation that will again return us to the emotional state that feels so familiar. Even though that state of familiarity might not be what we truly want to experience, it is appealing to the nervous system for its sense of familiarity, comfort, and predictability.

Later on in this workbook, we will also explore how certain emotional patterns first become neurologically wired during our early lives. For now, it is just important to understand that our emotional wiring does first occur during childhood, and that even the emotions that surface for us in the present moment are often a manifestation of experiences, and the resulting emotions, that were neurophysiologically recorded and stored in the past.

As a metaphorical example, let's say that a person is asked to open a door without knowing what is on the other side, and she suddenly experiences a profound, visceral fear that there may be a large tiger on the other side who, once the door is opened, might attack her.

Is this fear justified? Is it rational? Most likely, it is not. That is, there would be very few environments in which having a free-roaming wild tiger behind a door would make sense or be a rational possibility.

However, is her fear valid? Yes, it absolutely is.

Perhaps, as a child, this person had a traumatic experience at a zoo, saw something scary about tigers on television before her mind could cognitively process the information accurately, or maybe was even bitten by a domesticated animal, and her subconsciously stored past experience is now becoming exaggerated in the face of the unknown.

Regardless of the reason for this particular emotional response, the point here is that, since emotion is recorded, stored, and habitual, we may very often experience emotions that do not seem to make logical sense in the present moment.

In these cases, though, it is still necessary that we embrace and validate these emotions. For if we only allow ourselves to fully feel emotions that we think "make sense," we end up suppressing countless others.

We can only release emotional build-up by becoming aware of our feelings, and we can only become more aware of our feelings by allowing ourselves to feel them, whether or not we think they make sense.

Awareness of our stored and habituated emotional patterns is critical to transcending them, and thus to achieving our highest potential; for when we possess this awareness, we can begin to take steps towards positively rewiring our neurophysiological and behavioral patterns by reprogramming our nervous systems towards new, healthier states of being.

This kind of positive reprogramming of course requires consistent practice, patience, and a vast amount of self-compassion.

BOX: PRACTICE & REFLECTION PRINCIPLE #4

Feelings are NOT Always Rational—They are Habitual Records of the Past.

Given that feelings are habitual, for each of us there tend to be a few that we experience most consistently. Even becoming aware of what these habitual feelings are, and naming them, can be helpful in the process of rewiring our nervous systems for new patterns, and therefore for catalyzing personal growth.

Think about and write down the answers to the following questions:

1. What are the top three emotions or general feelings that you observe yourself experiencing on the most regular basis? For example: when you observe your inner state of being, is there most often a sense of feeling annoyed, sorry for yourself, unsettled, judged, afraid, helpless, ecstatic, content, peaceful, etc.? These are just some examples. What would you say are your top three "default" states of feeling, if you had to select just three?

2. How do you think these default states of habitual feeling might impact your experience of daily life in terms of how you see the world, certain situations, other people, and yourself?

3. How do you imagine you might relate differently to your own emotions if you really thought about them as merely condi-

tioned habits that you (like everyone else) unintentionally project onto certain situations in the present moment?

4. Given that feelings are a record of the past, and that they therefore may not always "make sense" in correlation to the present moment, have you ever had an experience where, in hindsight, you feel that the intensity of your emotional reaction did not truly match the current situation? Think about that time. What was the situation? What was your emotional reaction? Where do you imagine that emotional reaction might have stemmed from if it didn't match the present situation that was actually transpiring?

Simply thinking about the answers to these questions can sometimes bring greater awareness of the difference between our conditioning and our current, authentic selves.

You can also try writing down answers to fill in the following statements:

- The emotion(s) I felt during that situation were

  _____

- Another time I have felt this way (try to go back as early as you can remember) was when

  _____

- I see that these two situations might be related in the sense that _____

- I see that these two situations might bring up similar emotions because they both made me feel

  _____

(Here, you can insert various "untruths" that we all feel sometimes due to false unconscious programming—things we interpret about ourselves through the emotional lens of the child, but things that are not actually true—such as feeling *unloved, unworthy, not good enough, unseen, unheard, unimportant,* etc.)

- I know now that that's not true, though, and that I am in fact

_____

(Here, you can insert a bigger truth that rewrites that old false belief about yourself, such as *inherently worthy, good enough, loved, powerful, seen and heard, beautiful, autonomous, connected,* etc.)

Literally rewriting or restating new, healthier, and more accurate beliefs about ourselves can also help us overcome old patterns of emotional response by distinguishing to our subconscious minds the difference between false interpretations of past experiences created during the early developmental stages of a child's mind, and the truth about who we really are. This not only helps reduce emotional triggers in similar future situations that might other-wise bring up the same old emotional response patterns, it also helps us tap more deeply into our sense of true worth in the world in general, which is itself a catalyst for healing and transformation

Susan Kullman

Susan Kullman

CHAPTER TWO

EMOTIONAL AWARENESS: THE KEY TO SELF-EVOLUTION

"Your perception of the world is a reflection of your state of consciousness."

-EKHART TOLLE

Susan Kullman

A SIGNIFICANT QUESTION TO CONSIDER before going further into this work is: *why is learning a new language of emotion important?*

The answer is this: cultivating a deeper level of awareness regarding our relationship to our own emotions is essential to our personal growth. In order to embrace new ways of being, and therefore to achieve what we desire in life, we have to be aware of the role of our emotions in this journey.

Often, it is the case that we may know what we need to do in order to evolve to a new level of living, and yet our emotions seem to block our forward movement in that direction. This is because so many of our emotions, these deep and often unconscious vibrations, remain masked and hidden from our own view, from our own understanding. And it is when our emotions remain hidden from our conscious understanding that they acquire the power to generate blocks to our personal growth. In order to move past these blocks, the most powerful tool we can harness is our own emotional awareness.

DISMANTLING DISCOMFORT:
SEPARATING STORY FROM VIBRATION

In the first chapter, we explored a little bit about getting comfortable with discomfort by integrating some important *Guiding Principles about Feelings*, and by learning to distinguish between the ego and the witness.

Now that we have explored becoming *comfortable* with discomfort, we are going to take a look at how to begin to actually *dismantle* our discomfort. This requires that we elevate our awareness even further, and one way to achieve this elevation is to integrate another key distinction: namely, the difference between our *stories* and our *feelings*.

The guiding principles in Chapter 1 brought to our attention the important difference between *thinking about* and *feeling* our emotions, and the ability of this distinction to help create objectivity in the way we perceive our emotions. The principles also shed light on the notion that any emotion we feel, while it may not make sense given the present moment circumstances, is an habituated pattern that began somewhere in our past. Being aware of this distinction can sometimes help us feel more comfortable with uncomfortable emotion, as it allows us to understand that a given emotion is pre-programmed, and does not mean something specific about who we are; rather, it is simply energy moving through us, and the more space we make for it to do so, the more readily it dissipates.

Now, we will focus more closely on this distinction between our stories and our feelings, examining how it can help us begin to dismantle the discomfort that often arises in the face of unpleasant emotions.

First, let's get clear on what we mean exactly by the word *story*. A story is a certain narrative that we carry in mind, both about our individual lives in their entirety, and about certain sections of our lives. We all have these life narratives that walk with us.

Sometimes these stories are neutral, meaning they do not bring up a significant amount of emotion when we think about ourselves through their lenses. Other times, these stories can be healing or helpful if they bring up empowering emotions that drive us forward in our lives.

Sometimes, though, these stories can also be harmful to us, when the way we perceive and think about them consistently gives rise to certain feelings that create blocks to our own expansion, growth, and forward movement in life.

Therefore, while our stories are in some sense the actual products of our life circumstances and experiences, the impacts those stories can have on us are actually the products of our thought forms *about* those stories—our ways of thinking about and perceiving our life experiences.

And these thought forms can then generate certain ways of feeling and being, which then impact how we create our current and future life experiences. Therefore, stories and feelings can easily become integrated in a cycle, one that either serves our forward movement and growth or one that inhibits it.

In order to deconstruct and interrupt cycles of story and feeling that do not serve us well, we must become present to the distinction between the stories themselves (and our default ways of thinking about them), and our present-moment emotions.

Perhaps the most important difference between our stories and our feelings is this: our stories about how we feel live solely in our minds, while our feelings themselves also live in our bodies.

When we experience a big, uncomfortable emotion, remembering that it is a visceral experience often makes it easier for us to fully allow ourselves the time and space to feel that emotion, rather than entangling it in a story that disempowers us and creates resistance to allowing the feeling to move through us completely.

In this way, integrating the important distinction between our stories and our feelings can help us begin to deconstruct our discomfort when it comes to experiencing uncomfortable emotions.

Susan Kullman

BOX: PRACTICE & REFLECTION

Dismantling Discomfort

Find a comfortable, safe, and quiet place to relax. Lie on your back with your feet planted on the floor. As your knees bend and point at the ceiling, keep each foot and knee on its own side, in line with each hip. Rest your palms on your lower abdomen at the front of your pelvis. Gently close your eyes and breathe normally.

Allow your awareness to turn within, and begin to sense your inner experience:

- Do you notice any chatter occurring in your mind?

- Do you notice any physical sensations like pressure, pain, or certain temperatures or textures?

- Do you notice places within where you are feeling light and mobile, or conversely, where you are holding and gripping?

- Can you feel your body adjusting to your current position?

Once you have taken time to notice these sensations, gently allow your focus to rest more on your trunk and spine than on the dialogue in your mind, and call to mind a recent experience that resulted in an uncomfortable emotion.

As you allow any dialogue about this situation to unfold in your mind, can you distinguish between that dialogue and the sensations arising from the emotion itself?

The dialogue or story you experience in your mind may never

disappear completely, as it is simply part of being human. However, as you allow your focus simply to rest, without judgment, on the sensations in your body, the sound of that dialogue will likely become progressively quieter with time.

Write down some reflections that come to mind after completing this exercise.

CLEARING THE WAY FORWARD: UNBLOCKING OUR EMOTIONS

If we look at our discomfort with uncomfortable emotions as a brick wall that stands between us and our unlimited potential, what we have done thus far to dismantle that wall still leaves some remnant debris that we must clear away in order to truly move forward. The distinction between stories and feelings, though critical, is not necessarily enough in and of itself to support us on the journey of navigating an entirely new relationship with our emotions.

Here are some additional skills we need to cultivate in order to forge a new relationship with our emotions, and thus with ourselves:

Recognize When We are Using the Ego Mind to Navigate

To make sure we are really feeling our emotions, we must be able to recognize when we are not. In Chapter 1, we defined the term *ego* as it is used in this workbook. If you need to refresh your memory, please refer back to that chapter before reading on. It is important to understand how this word is being used here, and specifically, to understand the notion that, while it is necessary to acknowledge when the ego is blocking us from self-growth, this does not mean that we should ever label the ego as "bad," for it can still serve us in many important ways.

That said, when we are in an ego mind state, we are most often thinking rather than feeling. Therefore, the ego does *not* help us to develop a deeper relationship with our emotions; it cannot, for it is not the correct tool to use in this endeavor. It is analogous to trying to use a screwdriver to put a nail in the wall: fruitless, or at the very least, inefficient. The thinking intellect is incredibly important for accomplishing certain tasks, but it is *not* helpful for all tasks. At some point, we need to be able to identify and connect with what we feel, and in order to do this, we have to first recognize when we are in our *thinking mind*.

So, what are the characteristics of our ego, or thinking mind? It helps even just to be able to identify when we have shifted into an ego mind state, because it is only from that place of awareness that we can invite ourselves back to fully feeling our emotions from our core. Here are a few common tell-tale signs that we have entered an ego mind state, and thus may not be fully feeling our emotions:

- *Analyzing*: trying to figure out a given situation to see if you have a right to feel the way you do, or to explain it to yourself; trying to make sense of an overwhelming situation solely by using the mind

- *Having difficulty being fully present*: focusing on thoughts about the past or future, or overthinking about the present moment, rather than fully taking in the experiences and sensations of the present moment.

- *Rationalizing*: e.g., telling yourself that other people are in worse situations than you are, and that you should therefore not feel the way you do, etc.

- *Denial*: entering into a state of ignoring or excluding unpleasant feelings from unconscious awareness.

- *Minimizing*: e.g., telling yourself that you are being overly sensitive, etc.

- *Feeling thrown into a state of confusion*

- *Blaming something or someone else for causing your feeling*

- *Trying to be perfect*

- *Self-pity*

- *Procrastination*

- *Becoming suddenly overly tired:* feeling almost as if overcome by a chemical substance

- *Paralysis or non-action*

- *Judging:* labeling your thoughts or emotions, or others' thoughts or emotions, as good, bad, right or wrong.

- *Narration:* going through one or multiple stories in your mind that you have correlated with the way you're feeling

BOX: PRACTICE AND REFLECTION

Recognizing the Ego Mind

Take a look at the list above. While you may likely relate to all of them, since all humans do these things, try to identify one or two of the patterns you feel that you default towards the most, and write down a few real and tangible examples of times your ego mind has engaged in these kinds of habits.

Remember: our ego minds are *not* bad, they are just part of us that aims to protect us, though sometimes in ways that are no longer the most helpful to us.

Start with just a few examples to begin the process of recognizing when the ego mind might be kicking into overdrive. Keep your examples simple and few, as the goal here is not to overwhelm yourself, which can defeat the purpose of this exercise, but rather simply to begin to develop the skill of basic awareness. Make sure you also remember to remain as self-compassionate as possible during this exercise.

Practice Transmuting the Energy of Our Emotions

What we do not allow ourselves to feel, we inadvertently hold onto. It is much healthier and more helpful to use our energy to allow an emotion to come to full fruition and release, rather than to use that very same energy to repress, minimize or analyze it. When we choose the latter route, we inevitably remain attached to the story behind the emotion, rather than move through the vibration and use its energy to create something new in our lives.

This movement towards the new helps overcome stagnation and even disease. When we have a very high but equally suppressed vibration in our bodies, it can often manifest as inflammation and physical imbalance, as well as emotional imbalance. Rather than put ourselves through these challenges, it is much simpler just to take a short time to truly feel what we feel.

Because most of us have not had instilled in us that to feel our emotions fully is actually *easier* than to avoid or suppress them, we have to practice allowing ourselves to fully feel our feelings in order to see and believe that it is, in fact, an easier path. The more we practice this and see positive results, the more we build the unconscious muscle that allows us to feel without suppressing. Each time we practice this, we forge this new neural pathway a little bit further—a pathway that positively entrains us to know it is safe and healthy to feel what we feel.

So now that we have identified some skills we need in order to help unblock our emotions, let's look at *how* to actually practice doing that. It's one thing to *understand* that it's important to fully feel our feelings, but since for most of us our old habits of suppression and avoidance are deeply ingrained at the neurological level, it is quite another thing to actually allow ourselves to feel our emotions in a new way. Essentially, we have to completely re-learn how to experience our feelings, and in order to do that, we have to provide for ourselves a safe, gentle, and compassionate space where we can be authentic and vulnerable.

The most powerful way to do this is through the process of self-validation. As we touched on in the guiding principles in Chapter 1, all feelings—without exception—are valid. Putting this notion into action, a simple yet powerful way to create safe space for ourselves to fully experience our emotions is to actively practice validating them. The following practice, *The N's of Validation*, can help us do this.

Susan Kullman

BOX: PRACTICE & REFLECTION

Skill Building Practice: The Three N's

The tendency to block our emotions causes us to disconnect from ourselves, yet also cyclically arises *from* this disconnect. Therefore, in order to unblock our emotions, we must forge a radical reconnection with ourselves, and one of the best ways to do this is through the sincere validation of our own feelings.

The 3 N's of Validation is an exercise that helps integrate the reality that every single emotion you feel is: 1) normal, 2) natural, and 3) necessary.

While practicing the following validation exercises, notice if you unintentionally start to cross the threshold of validation into intellectual ego defenses like analysis or blame; if you do, try to gently invite yourself back to focusing on the validation itself. The purpose of this practice of self-validation is to help the ego feel safe enough to *release* its defenses so that we can adopt a more objective perspective when it comes to our own emotions, and therefore fully feel the vibration of each one.

In time, not only does this help us forge a radical reconnection with ourselves by allowing us to be authentically who we are, it also paves the way for potentially transformative insights to arise—for it is only when we allow ourselves to experience our emotions completely that we gain access to the deeper messages that they carry.

1. Normal

As we learned earlier, there is not a single emotion that is right, wrong, good or bad. All feelings just *are*. Every emotion you will ever experience—regardless of what, why, or when—will always be completely normal. This is because every emotion you feel arises from connections and correlations with past experiences, ways of thinking and feeling that you developed during childhood. This is the case for everyone.

So, the first validation you can practice offering yourself whenever you feel any emotion at all, is that what you are feeling is completely **normal**.

Try saying to yourself some natural variation of the following phrases, and fill in the blanks according to your own personal experience:

What I am feeling is completely normal.

It is completely normal that I feel (or felt) _____ when/because _____, given my past experiences.

Anyone who has experienced what I have in my past would feel _____ when _____.
It is normal and safe to feel this _____.

Here is an example, to get you started:

What I am feeling is completely normal.

It is completely normal that I feel <u>sadness</u> because <u>my job has ended</u>, especially given my past experiences.

Anyone in my position would feel <u>sadness</u> because of <u>a job ending</u>, especially if they have experienced what I have in my past. It is normal and safe to feel this <u>sadness</u>.

2. Natural

As we have also learned, all emotions arise in the body as visceral vibrations of energy. They are an organic and biological aspect of human experience, and this is the case for everyone.

It is important that when we experience an emotion, we also identify how it feels in the body so that we can validate that visceral experience, as well as the emotion itself. For example, if we experience a physical feeling of heat whenever we feel angry, it is important to validate that both the anger itself and the heat that accompanies it are natural, organic experiences.

So, the second validation you can practice offering yourself whenever you feel any emotion at all, is that what you are feeling—the emotion itself as well as its accompanying visceral sensations—is completely *natural*.

Try saying to yourself a variation of the following phrases, and fill in the blanks according to your own personal experience:

What I am feeling is completely natural.

It is natural and organic that I feel this _____.

In my body, I feel/sense _____, *and this is also natural, organic, and safe.*

Here is an example, to get you started:

What I am feeling is completely natural.

It is natural and organic that I feel this <u>sadness</u>.

In my body, I sense a <u>heavy feeling in my stomach</u>, and this is also natural, organic, and safe.

3. Necessary

All feelings have something to teach us. Every emotion we experience is necessary to feel in order to move through that particular phase of our growth, and to reap the rewards of fully processing the emotion. Such rewards may take the form of a positive shift in our emotional state to one of greater ease and balance, a redirection and freeing of the energy previously used to suppress or avoid our emotions, and new clarity about ourselves or the situations we face. These are rewards that often arise only when we process and experience our emotions completely.

Therefore, as a final powerful step in the process, the third validation you can practice offering yourself whenever you feel any emotion at all, is that what you are feeling is a **necessary** part of your growth and healing.

Try saying to yourself a variation of the following phrases:

Whatever I'm feeling right now, it is necessary to allow myself to fully feel it.

It is necessary and safe to allow myself to fully feel this _____ in order to grow, heal, and transform. I think it might help me do that by _____.

Here is an example, to get you started:

Whatever I'm feeling right now, it is necessary to allow myself to fully feel it.

It is necessary and safe to allow myself to fully feel this <u>sadness</u> in order to grow, heal, and transform. I think it might help me do that by letting me <u>mourn the ending of my job (even if I felt I actually wanted it to end), because it will give me closure and allow me to open up to new beginnings and opportunities.</u>

*Important note: please know that there is a critical difference between stating that feeling uncomfortable emotions is necessary because we somehow deserve to feel unhappy or uncomfortable (which, of course, we don't), and stating that it is necessary to feel uncomfortable emotions in order to move through our discomfort to the new levels of growth and healing that we deserve.

A New Road: Behavior Change

As we retrain ourselves to fully feel our emotions by validating them, and as we create the safe space needed to forge new neurological pathways, we lay the foundations for healthier patterns of behavior.

Whenever we set out on a path of personal growth in any domain, it is extremely helpful for enduring motivation to have some kind of gauge for measuring progress. This is goal-setting science. Being able to measure our own progress inspires us to continue moving forward on the path of growth and change.

It is important to recognize that behavioral change is never linear. However, as human beings, we do tend to measure things linearly—such as objects, time, and even ourselves—in order to try to understand them. Rulers, scales, and bank accounts are just some of the measuring tools we use to make sense of our world at a certain level. These types of measurements are concrete, and easy to see on paper.

When we are interested in behavioral shifts, the re-patterning of our relationship to our own emotions, and our ultimate personal growth, the tools and gauges of measurement are not always as clear. In fact, this is one of the primary reasons many people abandon the path of personal change and succumb to the illusion of disempowerment.

However, there *are* systems of measurement we can use when it comes to understanding our inner worlds and the very real outer shifts that result from change within. This does not mean that these forms of measurement encompass everything there is to know about this realm of transformation, yet they can still be helpful in tracking our progress to some extent, and therefore, in helping us stay motivated to keep going.

To understand how the brain and nervous system respond to emotional change is dependent upon understanding three particular forms of measurement. These forms of measurement are: duration, frequency, and intensity.

Duration

- *Duration is the amount of time something lasts.* When it comes to emotional, neurophysiological, and behavioral change, it can specifically refer to the amount of time we remain in a state of high uncomfortable emotional intensity following a triggering situation or event. Ten minutes shows progress from ten hours, which shows progress from 10 days, and so on.

Frequency

- *Frequency is the amount of times that something occurs.* In the realm of emotional, neurophysiological, and behavioral change, it can specifically refer to the number of times in a day or week that we experience a state of high uncomfortable emotional intensity following a triggering situation or event. Once per week shows progress from three times per week, which shows progress from every day of the week, and so on.

Intensity

- *Intensity is the degree to which something occurs.* In the realm of emotional, neurophysiological, and behavioral change, it can specifically refer to the degree to which we feel an uncomfortable emotion following a triggering situation or event. Feeling a low intensity of uncomfortable emotion following a given situation or event shows progress over feeling a higher degree of intensity following the same kind of event, and so on. The level of intensity with which we experience our emotions can then often impact our outward behavior and ability to communicate in those moments.

It is extremely important to understand that when using these tools of measurement in the delicate arena of self-growth, we must be very careful not to place judgment on ourselves if we find that we are at a point on the path where we experience uncomfortable emotions often, for long durations, or at high intensities.

We *never* want to pretend to experience anything different than what we are authentically experiencing, or to criticize ourselves for our authentic experience. We only want to use this knowledge as a gauge to measure our progress so that we know that we are in fact making noticeable changes at the level of our emotions, behaviors, and nervous systems.

These tools of measurement are to be used *only* as markers of where we are, and should never be used as fuel for self-criticism or suppression, which are of course two of the primary harmful habits we are aiming to shift.

Understanding how to measure personal progress in the realm of behavior change in terms of duration, frequency, and intensity can instead offer us encouragement, motivation, and support as we clear the way for a new road to emerge. We can track these three categories both with old behaviors that we wish to eradicate, as well as with new behaviors that we are aiming to achieve. Measuring our progress in this way offers us the following rewards:

- It gives us a measurable gauge that can keep us motivated as we see the arrow on each of these three scales move in a positive direction.

- It helps us not to be so hard on ourselves during the journey of growth, since it enables us to more distinctly notice even small steps of progress in each of these three areas.

Importantly, on any path of personal evolution and behavior change, we cannot become overly attached to old comfort zones. We must be willing to courageously dive into the river of transformation, thus breaking free of old patterns and into a new way of being. It is imperative, of course, that we have the right support network around us when we take these brave leaps, since they often require unraveling many years of deeply ingrained patterns.

Susan Kullman

Susan Kullman

CHAPTER THREE

THE PROCESS OF
FEELING OUR FEELINGS

"The process of feeling our feelings is something that we do for ourselves, with ourselves, and by ourselves."

- SUSAN KULLMAN

Susan Kullman

FEELING OUR FEELINGS IS A sacred act. No matter what they are, when they arise, and whether we perceive or label them as enjoyable, uncomfortable, or even distinctly undesirable. All such descriptors are just that: perceptions, labels, and assignments of value to certain emotions in favor of others. In fact, however, all of our emotions can teach us something significant; each one serves a purpose and carries a key to our own healing, growth, and transformation.

Of course, when it comes to feelings we perceive as positive, it is typically easy for us to embrace and appreciate them, as the human condition entails a predisposition to move towards pleasure and away from pain. However, when our goal is to do evolutionary work—in other words, when we aim to move beyond our personal histories, and to create ways of being that are new, both to ourselves and to the world at large—we must also cultivate our ability to embrace the uncomfortable.

One important component of learning to navigate discomfort, is the release of judgment in favor of awareness. Taking into account the guiding principles we explored in Chapter 1, a healthy relationship with our emotions asks us to decrease the brain's prefrontal cortex activities of thinking and categorizing, and instead simply to sit with our feelings, to be with them, to accept them, to validate them, and even just to notice them. This act of simply being present with our emotions, instead of analyzing or assessing them, both harnesses and impacts the brain in a very different way. Making this singular shift away from judgment and towards awareness can profoundly transform the way we engage with our emotions, with ourselves, and with the world.

Relating to our emotions from a place of awareness, rather than thinking and analysis, allows us to more easily embrace emotions we may have previously labeled as "bad," judged, or categorized in some other way; it ultimately allows us to see with greater clarity that our emotions do not necessarily *mean* anything about us. They reveal only our stories and interpretations, and given that these feelings can change as our thoughts and perceptions change, they clearly do not define who we are.

In order for us to build this kind of authentic emotional connection with ourselves, and then with others, we must find a way to pause. We must be willing to *just be* with our emotions from a place of objective awareness, rather than enmeshment with them.

To clarify, to be *enmeshed* with our emotions is to have little or no space between our awareness and our feelings themselves. This means that when something triggers our emotions, we become instantly caught up in a vortex of intensity that tells us, in that moment, that what we think and feel is the only truth. It means that our interpretation of those thoughts and feelings remains confined to one point of view, and, since our experiences of emotions are habitual records of the past, it is likely one of only a few perspectives that we have ever consciously known.

In short, to be enmeshed with our emotions means to believe that whatever we feel is in fact solely a product of our present moment experience, rather than what it actually is—a vibration intricately connected to a lifelong series of experiences, interpretations, and deeply wired neural connections. When we are enmeshed with our emotions, we identify with them as being *who we are*.

When we engage in the evolutionary process of self-transformation from a place of awareness rather than enmeshment, we instead recognize that, on the contrary, we *have* emotions and feelings, but they are not *who we are*.

One extremely important way we can experience this truth is simply to witness our emotions' corresponding vibrations in the body, until each one has been completely and viscerally processed, and therefore begins to lose its original level of intensity or to *neutralize its charge*.

When we focus on allowing our emotions to move through us in this way, it helps us stay present to the feeling rather than thinking about, analyzing, judging, or suppressing it. Also, by practicing this way of being with our emotions, we demonstrate to ourselves its actual effectiveness, for we come to see that no matter what our story is in the mind, when we allow emotions to move fully through the body, they will always dissipate and neutralize much more rapidly.

Learning to fully feel our feelings is a very unfamiliar and vulnerable process for most people, as it is not typically how we are taught to engage with emotions in our culture. Much more often, we are encouraged, or even required, to suppress our emotions in order to adapt to and survive in the world around us.

Therefore, the process of becoming more intimate and authentic with our own emotions can certainly trigger our protective minds to put up some initial barriers. That's okay. In the next section, we will learn about some of the primary emotions and the rewards that engaging more deeply with them can bring.

UNDERSTANDING & ENGAGING THE HEALING POTENTIAL OF THE PRIMARY EMOTIONS

When it comes to fully experiencing our emotions, there is one universal obstacle: the ego. As we explored in Chapter 1, our egos can greatly support our ability to navigate in the world, and yet, if we keep the ego engaged while trying to evolve past previous personal limitations in the realm of emotional experience, it is akin to using a screwdriver to hammer that nail into the wall; it's the wrong tool.

The way our egos often show up, in addition to thinking about and analyzing emotions instead of feeling them, is in the form of fear or resistance. It is normal that we may sometimes feel afraid of or resistant to fully feeling our emotions, especially if we learned or interpreted at an early age that it was either useless, unacceptable, or unsafe to feel or express our emotions. These outdated and yet neurologically wired patterns can block us from allowing ourselves to feel these emotions even now.

Also, when we hold a very large amount of a particularly old, unprocessed emotion, it can often feel too overwhelming to let ourselves experience it, and we may therefore continue to suppress the emotion until we no longer even consciously feel it.

Our egos keep us in this mode of either judging or bracing against our emotions in a well-intentioned effort to protect us, and yet, unless there is still an actual threat to our safety in the present environment, this is a false protection. In the realm of emotional experience, our true well-being almost always rests in our ability to lean all the way into our emotions, a task that only *the witness* can help us accomplish.

In Chapter 2, we explored the importance of validation, and practiced different ways to validate every one of our emotions. Sometimes, though, our emotional experiences can be quite complex and intertwined, making it difficult even to pinpoint what emotion we are actually experiencing, and often leading to a feeling of either numbness or overwhelm. In the following pages, we will unpack the various layers of some of the emotions most primary to human experience, so that we can begin to narrow in more closely on what we feel when we feel it.

We will explore the following aspects of each emotion:

- Common **signals** that indicate to us when we might be feeling a particular emotion; knowing these signals can help us more easily recognize when we are experiencing certain emotional states, thus heightening our sense of inner awareness.

- Possible **catalysts** for each emotion; understanding the underlying causes of our feelings can also help heighten our awareness and the ability to validate our emotions, thereby giving them more compassionate space to move through us completely.

- The **rewards** of processing each emotion; for all that inner work, there is always a profoundly positive and impactful result awaiting us on the other side of our efforts.

- Reflective **practices** that can be used to fully lean into and move through each emotion with greater ease and self-compassion.

As you go through the following pages, do your best to engage your personal witness, and also to use the 3N's of Validation, so that you can become more objectively present to each of these emotions without judgment. If your ego mind occasionally surfaces, that's okay—just gently return to the inner witness.

Keep in mind, also, that while it can be helpful to understand the catalysts of each emotion, it is best not to become overly focused on this aspect—the goal is to use this deeper understanding of the *why* to further allow yourself to feel what you feel, yet it is important not to get stuck in any intellectual analysis. Remember that it is not necessary to intellectually understand your feelings at all in order to give yourself permission to feel them, for as we know, every single feeling is always valid anyway. And even once you do understand a given emotion, it is still necessary to take the next step of letting go and allowing yourself to feel it from a place of nonjudgmental, compassionate awareness.

This very process of authentically feeling your emotions can itself then help you to further understand your past, identify negative core beliefs, and give you the power to transcend old patterns and behavior in order to create the life you truly desire.

This is because, while unprocessed emotions can negatively impact us by disconnecting us from our natural body signals and inner wisdom, when we let go and just sit with the vibrations of our emotions until they completely move through us and neutralize, we enter a state of connection with ourselves from which grounded clarity, higher wisdom, and deeper perspective are much more likely to arise.

As you practice this new way of being with the following emotions, be as patient and compassionate with yourself as possible. If you need to take a break and come back to this later, allow yourself to do that.

It is also worth noting that the various levels of challenge or trauma that may have brought a given emotion into being for you correlate to the amount of self-compassion and patience it will require to bring the vibration of that emotion back to a neutral state. The more we have ingrained a particular emotional pathway in our nervous systems, the more time it may take for that emotion to neutralize when it arises.

Also, sometimes we may not even realize we are feeling a particular emotion, if it is one that has been so commonplace for us that it feels almost "normal" or neutral itself. In this case, feeling our feelings requires that we first cultivate a heightened awareness that we *are* in fact feeling something. This, again, comes with time, practice, and quiet attention to our feelings. Make sure to go at your own pace, practice self-compassion, and take as many breaks as you need.

ANGER

Signal: Whenever you hear yourself blaming someone or something, or simply feeling a general sense of betrayal, this is usually an indication of unexpressed and/or unconscious anger.

Catalyst: Typically, a primary catalyst of anger is a boundary violation of any kind. Understanding the many layers of the concept boundaries requires in-depth study, one that could not possibly be covered in the span of this workbook.

However, here are just a few basic examples of potential boundary violations:

- Verbal or emotional harm (such as yelling or using abusive language)
- Physical harm
- Changing plans at the last minute
- Doing something one has been asked not to do
- Lying

- Having others assume they know how we feel without asking and listening

- Lack of clear communication

Sometimes, more often than we may realize in fact, we may even consciously or unconsciously violate our own boundaries. It is also normal to feel betrayed or angry at a part of yourself when you break your own boundaries.

Here are just a few examples of potential self-violated boundaries:

- Becoming distracted and therefore not following through on a commitment we made to ourselves

- Eating certain foods that we know make our bodies feel unwell

- Allowing others to influence our decisions in place of listening to our own intuition

- Suppressing our voices rather than fully speaking what we truly feel or believe

- Ignoring our own natural physical signals such as the need for sleep, rest, play, going to the bathroom, etc.

Reward of Processing Anger:

The reward of allowing ourselves to fully feel the vibration of anger is that, once this vibration is processed, we normally disengage the previously ingrained habit of allowing ourselves or others to cross the same boundaries again.

Anger can also be an extremely useful energy that propels us into action. When we truly feel our anger, the high intensity charge behind that emotion eventually neutralizes; the seemingly dangerous feeling of rage begins to weaken as we practice feeling our anger, thereby creating a new state of groundedness and safety. These new states of being then allow us to think, speak, and act differently.

Also, since by processing our anger we are simultaneously releasing formerly suppressed life force energy, fully feeling this emotion can also help reduce feelings of depression, and heighten feelings of vitality and joy. It is therefore necessary and healthy to allow ourselves to feel anger and to find non-harmful ways of expressing it.

Practice:

- Try asking yourself: *"What am I really angry about?"* or *"What wrong do I feel has been done to me?"* or *"If there is nothing and no one to blame, what is there?"*

- Try closing your eyes and visualizing yourself as a young child who needs compassion. Give that child the space he or she needs to feel this anger without judgment, in a container of unconditional safety and self-compassion. As you sit and allow the anger to exist, see if you can practice just observing it from above rather than becoming ensconced in it. Simply witness the flame of anger, and try to sit beside it until the embers glow and dissolve.

SADNESS

Signal: Whenever you notice that you are feeling a sense of loneliness or abandonment, this is usually an indication of unexpressed and/or unconscious sadness.

Catalyst: Typically, a primary catalyst of sadness is when something is ending or changing. Endings are naturally sad, since comfort zones, whether functional or dysfunctional, are just that: comfortable.

Therefore, it is normal to feel loss or sadness when:

- Something ends or changes, even when we may want it to end or change

- We create something new and leave something else behind, even when what we have created may be healthier and more fulfilling than what we leave behind.

Reward of Processing Sadness:

The reward of allowing ourselves to fully feel the vibration of sadness is that, once this vibration is processed, we are more able to allow ourselves to remain fully open to the potential and excitement of new beginnings, thus usually creating even more of them, and thereby transcending past personal limitations in exchange for self-evolution and growth.

Practice:

- Try asking yourself: *"What has ended or stopped recently?"* or *"What is changing right now?"*

- Try closing your eyes and visualizing yourself as a young child who needs space to feel. Give that child the space he or she needs to feel this sadness without judgment, in a container of unconditional safety and self-compassion.

FEAR

Signal: Whenever you notice that you feel anxiety or a general sense of uncertainty, this is usually an indication of a deeper unexpressed and/or unconscious fear.

Catalyst: Typically, a primary catalyst of fear is uncertainty, and/or when your mind perceives a need to warn you about something it has interpreted as being dangerous (whether it actually is or not).

Reward of Processing Fear:

When we really allow ourselves to process the vibration of fear, we become much more open to our body's unique warning signals. We also develop the ability to distinguish between real and perceived threat, and therefore to know how to proceed using our innate wisdom to make decisions about our responses.

When we allow ourselves to fully feel the emotion of fear, we transform our anxiety, which is an ungrounded vibration that can often lead us to think, speak, or act in undesirable ways. Instead, we become aware of "warnings" in a grounded, neutral energy that yields thought, words, and actions that are much more clear and helpful, no matter the situation at hand.

Practice:

- Try asking yourself: *"What am I afraid of?"* or *"What am I believing to be true right now?"* or *"What is this fear trying to warn me of?"*

- Try closing your eyes and visualizing yourself as a young child who needs acceptance. Give that child the space he or she needs to feel this vibration of fear without judgment, in a container of unconditional safety and self-compassion

SORROW

Signal: Whenever you notice that you feel indifference toward people or life, or have a sense of powerlessness, this is usually an indication of unexpressed and/or unconscious sorrow.

Catalyst: Typically, a primary catalyst of sorrow is desiring something beyond reach. Sorrow, like sadness, also tends to arise when something ends, yet it differs in that it is also often accompanied by feelings of powerlessness. These feelings can arise when we desire something that most likely can never be. This is often a relic tendency of the inner child, who may have always longed for something outside the limitations of his or her childhood experience—for example, a certain kind of relationship with someone who was simply not capable of it, healing of a loved one with chronic illness, greater reconciliation or recovery after a collective trauma such as a natural disaster, or to take back control over anything that is naturally beyond our control.

Reward of Processing Sorrow:

It is necessary to process the vibration of sorrow and to give ourselves permission to grieve loss. Again, this loss may be the actual death of someone close to us, yet it can also just be the feeling that we have not received, or cannot possibly receive, something that we have always longed for—this is also a kind of loss that brings grief with it.

Grief itself is actually the benefit of processing sorrow, for although grief may not seem like a positive thing, when we do not allow ourselves to fully experience grief, we can instead become guarded and experience feelings of indifference even to those we love. Conversely, allowing ourselves to feel the often uncomfortable emotion of deep sorrow and its resulting sense of grief also allows us to experience a much deeper feeling of true connection with those we love.

Practice:

- Try asking yourself: *"What did I always want and never received?"* or *"What has changed forever?"*

- Try closing your eyes and visualizing yourself as a young child who needs acceptance. Give that child the space he or she needs to feel this sorrow without judgment, in a container of unconditional safety and self-compassion.

FRUSTRATION

Signal: Whenever you notice that you are judging yourself, or feel a general sense of dissatisfaction, this is usually an indication of unexpressed and/or unconscious frustration.

Catalyst: Typically, a primary catalyst of frustration is when a certain process is taking longer than we expect or want it to. Often, we feel this frustration when we are not giving ourselves the time and space we need to grow. It is common, as part of the human condition, to think in terms of all or nothing, yet true change tends to occur in incremental and sometimes nearly invisible steps, so we might often feel that nothing is happening when, in fact, it is.

Reward of Processing Frustration:

When we allow ourselves to fully feel the vibration of frustration, we thereby diminish the urge to react with "all or nothing" thinking. Allowing frustration to process through us completely helps us to persist with patience, consistency, and endurance when things take longer than expected.

Practice:

- Try asking yourself: *"What is taking longer than I expected?"*

- Try closing your eyes and visualizing yourself as a young child who needs acceptance. Give that child the space he or she needs to feel this frustration without judgment, in a container of unconditional safety and self-compassion. Encourage your inner child to release the pressure of certain life processes, remembering that all of life itself is a process, and even that which seems like a "mistake" or "hindrance" on our timelines can help us grow on our journey.

DISAPPOINTMENT

Signal: Whenever you are having a hard time making a decision or feel a general sense of discouragement, this is usually an indication of unexpressed and/or unconscious disappointment.

Catalyst: Typically, a primary catalyst of disappointment is when things do not go the way we wanted them to. Things often take more time, or require more focus, than we realize. The more expectations we have towards something, the more we typically position ourselves for disappointment.

Reward of Processing Disappointment:

When we allow ourselves the space to truly feel the vibration of disappointment, we are better able to release attachment to our desired outcomes, and thus allow space for something else to present itself to us. Truly processing life's disappointments allows us to surrender a narrow point of view, and therefore remain open to the unfolding of larger interconnected occurrences we may not have been able to conceive of on our own.

Practice:

- Try asking yourself: *"With what or whom am I feeling disappointed?"* or *"Is there an expectation of mine that is not being met?"*

- Try closing your eyes and visualizing yourself as a young child who needs acceptance. Give that child the space he or she needs to feel this disappointment without judgment, in a container of unconditional safety and self-compassion.

WORRY

Signal: Whenever you notice yourself procrastinating or feeling a general sense of helplessness in a particular situation, this is usually an indication of unexpressed and/or unconscious worry.

Catalyst: Typically, a primary catalyst of worry is when we do not feel prepared for a project or task, or for whatever is coming next. Uncertainty on any level can create the vibration of worry. We also often experience worry when we assume or reach for control over things that are not possible to control, such as other people's actions.

Reward of Processing Worry:

Allowing ourselves to fully feel the vibration of worry can help us better prepare for things that are within our control, whereas when we try to block this feeling, it often leads us to remain frozen in a state of procrastination and unable to take the appropriate steps in order to move forward. Remember that allowing ourselves to simply feel the vibration of worry does not mean that we must first know what or how to prepare for our next steps. Processing the emotion itself will help clear the mind so that the appropriate response occurs much more naturally, with greater ease and clarity.

Practice:

- Try asking yourself: *"What am I worried about?"*

- Try closing your eyes and visualizing yourself as a young child who needs acceptance. Give that child the space he or she needs to feel this vibration of worry without judgment, in a container of unconditional safety and self-compassion. Allow him or her to feel the natural worry that tends to accompany the uncertainty of life, and possibly, to even begin to trust in the process of that uncertainty by releasing expectations of perfectionism.

EMBARRASSMENT

Signal: Whenever you experience feelings of inadequacy, or notice you are putting pressure on yourself to achieve something, or to be perceived as having achieved something—usually at a level of unattainable perfectionism—this often is an indication of unexpressed and/or unconscious embarrassment.

Catalyst: Typically, a primary catalyst of embarrassment is when we are not accepting something about ourselves in a given moment. Very often, we judge ourselves based on standards that have been deeply ingrained in us either by our caretakers or by our culture. When we become caught in a cycle of craving approval from others, this positions us for more frequent experiences of embarrassment than when we feel secure in our own core self-worth.

Reward of Processing Embarrassment:

Allowing ourselves to feel embarrassment when we make so-called "mistakes" or aren't exactly where we feel we "should" be in life, enables us to engage in greater levels of self-acceptance, rather than trying to attain an unachievable goal of perfection. There will always be more to do, or more to learn. When we can truly accept ourselves, appreciating our own unique complexities of experience, and when we can embrace *all* of who we are and *all* of our experience, and allow it to be ok, then we can genuinely nurture ourselves. And when we nurture ourselves at this authentic level, we can create new kinds of experiences that more nearly match the versions of ourselves we would like to embody, because we are already acknowledging our own self-worth, which is always infinite and naturally existent, independent of our perceived achievements.

Practice:

- Try asking yourself: *"What am I not accepting about myself, or the process of learning, at this moment?"* or *"Where am I not accepting my own humanness?"*

- Try closing your eyes and visualizing yourself as a young child who needs acceptance. Give that child the space he or she needs to feel this embarrassment without judgment, in a container of unconditional safety and self-compassion.

ENVY

Signal: Whenever you feel jealousy or resentment towards something, this is usually an indication of unexpressed and/or unconscious envy.

Catalyst: Typically, a primary catalyst of envy is the experience of unmet desire. We do not always recognize our desires; therefore, the feeling of envy can in fact be quite informative. If you find yourself either feeling deprived of a particular life experience, or feeling or expressing jealousy, negativity, or sarcasm when it comes to a particular situation or person, it is often because there is an underlying desire you have yet to acknowledge or give yourself permission to manifest in your life.

Reward of Processing Envy:

Instead of remaining in the uncomfortable energy of jealousy or deprivation, when we allow ourselves to fully feel our envy, it allows us to admit to ourselves our true desires—and when we can clearly own our feelings of desire, it is then that we can often take the appropriate steps to fulfill those desires ourselves, and thus to create the life we want and deserve.

Practice:

- Try asking yourself: *"What am I really feeling envious of?"* or *"What do I really want that this other person/situation has?"*

- Try closing your eyes and visualizing yourself as a young child who needs acceptance. Give that child the space and the permission he or she needs to feel this envy (as well as the permission to want what he or she desires) without judgment, in a container of unconditional safety and self-compassion.

HURT

Signal: Whenever you feel a sense of shame, feel sorry for yourself, or feel left out, this is usually an indication of unexpressed and/or unconscious hurt.

Catalyst: Typically, a primary catalyst of hurt is when we feel that someone has excluded us, or we perceive that they have somehow isolated us through an act of judgment, even if that judgment is nonverbal and not tangibly enacted. We also experience the vibration of hurt when we are judging ourselves, and not giving ourselves the necessary permission or acceptance to be different from others and to be authentically who we are. It is normal to feel the vibration of hurt when we are looking for validation externally.

Reward of Processing Hurt:

When we allow ourselves to fully feel the vibration of hurt, it often helps us to become aware of the source of our pain, for the ultimate purpose of healing it, rather than unintentionally slipping into a disempowering cycle of feeling sorry for ourselves or becoming immersed in shame. Giving ourselves the permission we need to feel the hurt completely allows us to move beyond it in order to fulfill ourselves in new, healthier ways. Allowing ourselves to fully process the vibration of hurt also offers the exceptionally healing opportunity to bring us into greater acceptance of our own unique and authentic individuality.

Practice:

- Try asking yourself: *"Is there something about myself or my own feelings that I might not yet be aware of or realize?"* or *"Where or how, specifically, am I feeling hurt?"*
- Try closing your eyes and visualizing yourself as a young child who needs acceptance. Give that child the space he or she needs to feel this hurt (as well as permission to experience the unique level of sensitivity with which he or she naturally came into the world) without judgment, in a container of unconditional safety and self-compassion.

APPREHENSION

Signal: Whenever you feel confused or a sense of hopelessness, this is usually an indication of unexpressed and/or unconscious apprehension. In this workbook, apprehension is distinct from fear in its element of underlying excitement or anticipation (such as when starting something new or unknown, for example), rather than panic or a more deeply seated sense of fear.

Catalyst: Typically, a primary catalyst of apprehension is when we begin something new—e.g., the first day of school or a new job—as beginnings can be naturally scary.

Reward of Processing Apprehension:

When we resist fully feeling apprehension, we may instead often notice a sense of confusion on the surface, which immobilizes us and inhibits our ability to engage with and learn from new experiences. On the other hand, when we allow ourselves to fully feel the vibration of being apprehensive, we become much more likely to remain open to new experiences, and to greet them with both curiosity and creativity.

Practice:

- Try asking yourself: *"What am I scared about?"* or *"Is there something unknown or uncertain that I am experiencing?"*

- Try closing your eyes and visualizing yourself as a young child who needs acceptance. Give that child the space and permission he or she needs to feel this apprehension without judgment, in a container of unconditional safety and self-compassion. Try offering your inner child the knowledge that new beginnings are scary for everyone, and also that it is normal to experience sensations of fear and excitement at the same time.

Becoming more *aware* of our emotions, rather than *entangled* in them—no matter what they are—allows us to move through them with greater ease, and therefore to facilitate more conscious personal growth.

There is an important clarification to be made regarding what it specifically means to *move through* our feelings. Many people speak about emotions in terms of "releasing" them. The conceived goal, in this case, is to feel the emotion and then, as soon as possible, not to feel it anymore. While it may be reasonable to want to release uncomfortable emotions, the fastest and most efficient way to move through them is, perhaps somewhat counterintuitively, to dive into them completely and to experience them to their fullest.

When we do this, not only do we build tolerance to being present to discomfort in a way that can heighten our sense of inner peace and diminish our fears around unpleasant emotions, we also create a necessary space for the emotion—a moving, organic vibration of energy—to unfold according to its own natural energetic lifespan. If the emotion needs to carry a certain energy through to fruition in order to dissipate and leave the body, then making space for it to fully come to life actually allows for its quicker disintegration and a more rapid return to a stable, peaceful energy point.

On the other hand, although the concept of *releasing* a feeling might sound positive, oftentimes what we call release is actually, on the contrary, either an unintentional or unconscious act of avoidance or suppression. We often say, for example, that we are letting go of an emotion, when instead what we are really doing is pushing it into the background; in doing so, we deny emotion the space it needs to fully be what it is, and we therefore actually end up prolonging its duration.

It is well-known in the field of psychology that emotions we suppress can become stored in the mind and body, and can continue for years, even decades, to create imbalance, unrest, and disease—both physical and psychological. This is because emotions generate energy, and as science dictates, energy can never die—it can only be transformed.

Similarly, our emotions do not disappear when we ignore them or push them away; although they may seem to fade, they only change shape and undergo metamorphosis into other manifestations and symptoms, both visible and invisible, tangible and intangible.

When we consciously allow uncomfortable emotions to exist in their fullest incarnations without judgment or fear, however—something that certainly requires both practice and patience—it takes exponentially less time for them to rise and fall. And in this more freely occurring rise and fall, our emotions often then leave even greater lessons, and ideally, a greater sense of inner peace in their wake.

BOX: PRACTICE & REFLECTION

Emotional Signals

For each of the emotional *signals* listed above, identify and write down a concrete example of a time when this feeling has arisen for you.

For each of the emotions and examples you wrote down, reflect on each of the *rewards* for processing that emotion (refer again to the list of rewards above), and write down some thoughts about how you imagine that fully processing each emotion might serve your personal growth and healing.

Now, pause to reflect on and write down the answer to this question:

How might thinking about your emotional experiences in the ways elucidated and framed in this chapter help you to become more objective, self-compassionate, and self-validating when it comes to your relationship with your own emotions?

Susan Kullman

Susan Kullman

Chapter Four

THE SOMATIC IMPACT OF EMOTIONS & THE EVOLUTIONARY VALUE OF RELAXATION

"As your feelings change, this mixture of peptides travels throughout your body and your brain. And they're literally changing the chemistry of every cell in your body."

-Dr. Candace Pert

Susan Kullman

THE WORD *SOMATIC* REFERS TO the element of experience that has to do with the physical body. Often, the use of this term is also correlated with the notion of the body's innate capacity to hold and process emotion, to harbor a certain kind of knowledge about its own needs and potentials for healing, and from that knowledge to offer us wisdom beyond that which our conscious thoughts are often able to generate.

Not only does our physiology possess the ability to impact us by delivering its own wisdom and feedback (which we can hear when we listen carefully), but we also possess the ability to impact our bodies based on how we process and experience our thoughts and emotions.

Often, of course, this processing and experiencing is largely unconscious and therefore beyond our immediate control, yet when we seek out, learn, and practice implementing tools for facilitating our own self-growth and self-awareness in this realm, we can then make more conscious choices about how to process and experience our emotions in a way that is not only psychologically and emotionally beneficial to us, but is also better for our physical bodies.

As highlighted in the quote above by Dr. Candace Pert, who was renowned for her work in the field of understanding how our emotions impact our bodies, all emotions release different chemical signals that impact every single one of our cells. With repeated release of the same chemical signals, and their correlative emotions, those chemical imprints on our cells become further and further ingrained, making it easier for us to experience those same emotions in the future.

Furthermore, when we do not allow ourselves to fully process our emotions, our bodies also experience a chemical impact that can result in a negative effect on our physical health.

EMOTION LIVES IN THE BODY

In the guiding principles in Chapter 1, we learned that when we block ourselves from experiencing our emotions, the vibrations, biological chemicals, and neurological pathways created by those blocked emotions begin to deeply impact not only our minds, but also our physical bodies. Blocked emotions can cause muscle tension, dysfunctional movement patterns, and reduced neuroplasticity (the brain's natural ability to change its neuronal connections for the purpose of healing and regeneration)—all of which are essential to our physical health and longevity, our mental stability, and our happiness. The effects of our emotions as they pertain to our physical bodies is their *somatic impact.*

This is a concept that is now quite well-known in the fields of neurobiology and the behavioral sciences, and has also recently become more acknowledged and integrated in the field of psychology as well. However, for those outside these fields of research, the concept of the somatic impact of emotions may sometimes seem less intuitive.

That is because, as we have explored, most of us tend to erroneously identify the stories behind our feelings with the feelings themselves. As we have seen, however, it is important to learn to distinguish between the story (which often arises from something that happened in the past) and the actual vibration or chemical flow of the emotion that is occurring in the moment we feel it. Another reason it is important to make this distinction between our stories and our emotions has to do with understanding the process behind somatic impact.

Specifically, in order to move beyond our personal limitations, and to achieve greater health and well-being, we must remember that our stories always live in the mind, while our emotions live in the *body*. To reduce negative impact on our bodies, therefore, we need to renegotiate a relationship with our emotions in which we allow ourselves to fully feel them, and therefore to allow them to process through our bodies in the freest way possible.

A natural question to ask in order to understand how to change our relationship to emotions is: why do we ever block our emotions to begin with? Of course, this is most often a completely unconscious decision, yet if it is so distressing to both the mind and the body, why would we even be unconsciously programmed to make such a choice?

The answer may vary slightly from person to person, but in general, the tendency to block our emotions comes from the early-life habit of protectively blocking experiences when certain things (or perhaps even many things, for some people) were too overwhelming for our nervous systems to fully experience. In humans, as with most other species, there is a natural tendency to brace against pain, which is an important survival mechanism.

However, it also prevents us from experiencing the emotions associated with the painful or traumatic event. While many other animal species naturally and immediately dispel the remaining vibrations of trauma from their bodies (for example, most animals allow their bodies to tremble following an overload of fear in the nervous system, even after the source of the threat has already gone away), humans have the tendency instead to remain to some degree in that state of braced protection, never fully allowing the vibrations to move through them and therefore to dissipate. When this prolonged state of bracing occurs, these vibrations then take long-term root in the body. Once they do so, their chemical imprints can create actual physiological changes at the cellular level.

Another important thing to understand about the somatic impact of suppressed emotions, is that it also affects something called *fascia*, which is a complex network of soft tissue that is completely interconnected in one system throughout the body. So even if we experience pain in one part of the body, it can often be the result of a problem somewhere else, as energy moves somewhat like water throughout the network of the fascia.

We all possess these water-like properties in the way that energy moves through our bodies; therefore, we can easily block the flow of this energy in unhealthy ways—such as when we ignore or avoid feeling our feelings—and yet, we also have the redeeming capacity to return to buoyancy and flow, especially when we fully allow our emotions to reach their natural level of vibration in the moment we experience them, instead of suppressing or blocking their movement. This is much healthier for every part of us—emotionally, psychologically, and physically.

BOX: PRACTICE & REFLECTION

Somatic Breathing Meditation

The following exercise is a somatic breathing meditation that you can practice in order to begin exploring the wisdom of your body.

It not only allows the body to move into a deeper relaxation response, but truly allows you to practice sensing *inside* your body, even visualizing beneath the level of the skin perhaps, so that you start to really feel your own experience from the inside-out.

Begin by lying on your back on the floor, with knees bent so that your feet are planted in line with your hips. Place your feet a comfortable distance away from your pelvis—close enough that there is minimal effort to hold your legs up, but far enough so that you maintain a neutral position in the pelvis, maintaining the slight natural lumbar curve of the spine. If your back is flattened completely to the floor, your feet are too close to your pelvis.

Next, contract your pelvic floor by using the same muscles you would if you were trying to stop the flow of urine, for example. This brings awareness to the pelvic floor, which is an important part of becoming more in tune with the body's groundedness and alignment.

As you lie on your back, envision your pelvic floor as a dome shape, and on your next exhalation, gently and without strain, lift the pelvic floor toward your navel—envision doing this as if you were exhaling from the pelvic floor itself.

As you lift the pelvic floor, see if you can sense the inside of your abdominal cavity begin to shrink inwardly towards your organs, almost as if your skin were moving closer to the bones of your ribcage.

Follow your exhale all the way to the end without strain, and as you approach the end of the exhalation, completely let go of all muscular effort and tension and simply allow a new breath to come into your body without any conscious involvement at all. Resist the urge to actively take a deep breath in—instead, simply *allow* the new breath to enter your body.

This inhale involves only your awareness and witnessing. Watch and allow the new breath to travel through your body and up your spine.

Give yourself at least twenty to thirty minutes to explore this breathing exercise, as it takes time and patience to really drop down fully into this new somatic exploration. Try to maintain a sense of presence, as in each breath cycle there is often something new to feel or discover.

Allow each inhale to be a rebirth-like experience, as new buoyancy and spaciousness enter the body. And see each exhale as an opportunity to fully draw all tension out of the body.

As you deepen into this exploration, you might even experience the illusionary sense of your physical body almost dissolving. Continue to trust the deeper and deeper layers of relaxing into this exercise as you extend your level of presence and awareness beyond your physical body, knowing that you are still grounded and safe in your physical environment.

Every single breath—in and out—offers a new ability to relax deeper into the expansive space of your inner body and to become immersed in the illumination of its wisdom.

WISDOM LIVES IN THE BODY

Just like emotions live in our bodies, so does some of our deepest unconscious wisdom. Our bodies are extremely intelligent mechanisms that are always trying to restore balance to their own ecosystems, and therefore, every single symptom we experience carries an important message with it. Our bodies can therefore be our most powerful teachers, as long as we learn to listen to and understand their language.

The language of the body, when it needs to return to homeostasis (balance), is communicated through what is known as *symptomatology*, which is a physical manifestation or expression of internal imbalance that signals a need for healing and restoration.

One of the most renowned fathers of modern psychology, Carl Jung, asserted that physical symptoms carry to us from our subconscious minds important wisdom about our need for emotional restoration, stating that "there is seldom a bodily ailment that does not show psychic complications, even if it is not psychically caused." (Jung, C. G., *Two Essays on Analytical Psychology*, second edition, translated by R. F. C. Hull, Routledge London, 1999.) Usually, once we resolve whatever emotional or psychological challenge lies at the root of a symptom, we may find that the symptom either dissipates or may even disappear altogether. Sometimes we are aware of this direct correlation, and many other times we are not. We just know that we feel better. This is not equivalent to saying that a symptom or physical feeling is "just in the mind." In fact, it is quite the opposite—it suggests instead that while something may begin in the mind (such as a pattern of emotion), it can eventually yield a very real physical impact on the body itself.

As we just explored in the previous section, suppressed emotion is so often the root cause of physical imbalance and "dis-ease." Whenever we experience any physical symptom, at least part of its message tends to be that we must allow ourselves to more fully feel a particular emotion or set of emotions so we can then positively alter their chemical impact on our cells and organs.

The opportunity this understanding offers us for potential growth, learning, and healing is a new lens through which we can now view our relationship with our emotions. Instead of avoiding or blocking our emotions at all costs, fully feeling them is in fact necessary for our own healing at every level of being human—the emotional, the psychological, and even the physical. Our bodies know this, and therefore "speak" to us when we need to return to a greater state of internal balance and wellbeing by more fully acknowledging and experiencing what we feel.

REPATTERNING FOR RELAXATION

Because the suppression of our emotions is most often the result of having received an unconscious message during our early lives that it was not safe for us to feel, relearning how to fully experience emotion is essentially equivalent to learning a new process of heightened nervous system relaxation.

In our modern culture, we tend not to place significant value on relaxation, as we often overlook that learning how to truly relax in fact possesses *evolutionary value.*

Evolutionary value is the degree to which something helps us to transcend past limitations—both individually, and once enough people adapt to it, also on a societal and global level. These larger scale adaptations can of course take decades and even centuries to transpire, but every change we make in our individual lives has the potential to impact this larger scale of change and evolution. And the bonus is that the changes we make in our own lives typically yield tangible and noticeable results in a much shorter time frame.

To rewire ourselves for a deeper and more automatic relaxation response (when appropriate to the safety level of the present environment), is to help further our own personal growth and evolution, and therefore to take one step closer to helping the world evolve as well. To reprogram our bodies and minds to fully relax—into ourselves, into our food, into our home, into our partner's eyes, into our friends and our children, into the earth, and into everything safe that surrounds us—is to literally rewire our brains to feel this deeper sense of safety in all of our environments and experiences. And when enough people begin to more naturally engage a sense of safety and relaxation in daily life, interactions begin to change; and changed interactions lead to changed societies.

Of course, there are many environments in our current society, especially for certain minorities or marginalized groups of people, that really do pose a threat to personal safety, either physically or emotionally. This is a different scenario that deserves more elaboration than can be granted in the scope of this workbook, yet it is a reality that needs to be acknowledged as we speak about engaging a deeper relaxation response. Sometimes, we really do need to harness our instinctive protective mechanisms. Again, though, practicing feeling our emotions also helps us hone in on our own instincts and helps us to know when an environment is safe or not.

However, even in environments that are actually safe, and even for those of us who do not typically need to confront present physical or emotional danger on a daily basis, it is still difficult for most of us to truly let go and relax. This is because of our early life programming, which for many of us has created a protective mechanism that means, even when we really are safe, we often do not *feel* safe enough to fully relax at the level of the nervous system.

We might even consciously think that we feel safe and are in a state of relaxation, yet our nervous systems may be enacting something completely different. Some, for example, grind their teeth during sleep because of this neurologically-ingrained program to brace against anything that is happening in the environment, even when the environment is completely neutral.

So how, then, can we undo this programming, and replace it with one that allows us instead to truly relax, and therefore to facilitate our personal growth? The answer lies in learning to trust the process of letting go, and in surrendering to this new practice of fully feeling our own emotions.

In order to trust this process, though, because it can be so difficult for so many, we must first truly understand and *feel* the value in this learning process. When we first begin to practice it, many uncomfortable emotions may rise to the surface because of so many years of suppressing them and thus storing them in the cells of the body. And especially if we have experienced trauma, it might be difficult to trust that letting go and feeling these emotions is actually safe.

While it is of utmost importance to always listen to ourselves, to be gentle with ourselves, and to have the right support network around us, in order to adopt new beliefs about our core safety that help transcend old patterns and limitations, we have to stick with it. This new kind of evolutionary relaxation takes practice, patience, and self-compassion.

When we unintentionally cut ourselves off from our emotions, we impose a block that prevents those emotions from completing their natural lifespan, and interrupts our neuromuscular pattern of feeling by superimposing a stronger pattern on top of it—one of suppression or diminishment. A block is also a neuromuscular pattern, and can manifest, for example, as muscular tension.

We all experience emotions in different parts of our bodies. Chronic pain or dysfunctional movement patterns (of the pelvis, neck, shoulder, etc.) therefore open the door for a different kind of inquiry around pain and disease in the body—one that helps us examine how we may be holding blocked feelings and patterns of suppression that we developed in order to survive a particular situation or period in our lives. However, as mentioned above, once a trauma has been survived and the harmful or negative stimuli are no longer present in our environment, we no longer have to hold that block. Now we can rest, knowing that in our current environment we are safe to relax.

To clarify, relaxation and trusting the process of letting go may not be *comfortable*, but with the right support network, it is safe.

It absolutely takes emotional courage to engage in a new pattern of trust and opening, but it is also absolutely possible. We have a choice. We can either teach ourselves repeatedly to brace against the negative, which then becomes a habit, a patterning in the brain and the body, *or* we can intentionally begin to *repattern* our minds for relaxation. We can begin to fully allow even our uncomfortable emotions to move through us.

So how can we start to undo our old patterns? We begin to repattern through a process of psychosomatic regeneration and integration by teaching ourselves a different experiential association to our emotions, one that is possible when we provide ourselves with a supportive way to process unprocessed feelings.

In doing so, we let our brains and bodies know that it is safe to feel. Then, once we allow ourselves to feel, and are therefore able to allow the vibration of our emotions to move through and out of the body, this in turn neutralizes the stories behind these emotions—and when we are in this more neutral state, we can then repattern even further. It is a positive cycle that we only need to begin in order to see it spiral in a healthy direction.

The more we surrender and allow ourselves to move through previously blocked emotions, the more we can actually allow in the *positive* emotions as well. In this way, we can rewrite our emotional, neurological, and physiological patterns, and thus enjoy a completely different experience in our present day lives.

Susan Kullman

BOX: PRACTICE & REFLECTION

Improving Mind-Body Connection

This exploration is an easy and simple way to improve your mind-body connection, mental focus and clarity. Try to approach this exploration with a sense of curiosity and ease.

Engaging in somatic meditation is a process of finding the place between doing and "non-doing."

This balance takes practice, so for now, just do your best to orient yourself to this exercise with alertness, yet without tension—with relaxation, yet without completely tuning out.

To begin, lie on the floor in a comfortable position, maybe supporting your body with a blanket or pillow(s) under your head and/or knees—whatever allows you to feel most at ease in your body.

As your body begins to relax further into the floor, begin simply to focus on the rise and fall of your breath. There is no need to change your breath in any way, only to become gently aware of it.

Now, starting at the top of your head and working your way all the way down to each finger and toe, consciously focus on trying to engage the muscles of the specific area where your attention is and then focus on consciously releasing the tension in that area. Continue to do this exercise as you move your awareness throughout the entire body.

If you lose your focus at any point, just pick up where you remember leaving off last.

Once you have gone through every part of your body in this way, continue laying in a comfortable position, and then, if it feels right for you, silently repeat the mantra, "It is safe to sense, relax and release".

Treat this just like any other meditation, both relaxing and remaining aware at the same time. Allow any mind chatter to be there without focusing on it, and instead continue to bring your awareness to the sensations in your body and continue to open, release, and relax.

Do your best to remain open-minded and curious about your individual experience, with no expectation of how you think this exploration should unfold.

Write down some reflections or insights that may have occurred to you during this exercise. Each time you engage in this exploration, your experience of connection to your body might change.

Susan Kullman

CHAPTER FIVE

SOFTENING FURTHER INTO FEELING

*"Instead of resisting any emotion,
the best way to dispel it is to enter it fully…"*

- DEEPAK CHOPRA

Susan Kullman

So far, we have taken a detailed look at the ways we often block ourselves from fully feeling our feelings, as well as some ways to objectively reflect on and shift that tendency. We have learned to recognize and address the signals that indicate when we have moved out of emotional vulnerability and have begun instead to build walls.

Sometimes these walls are thick and very obvious, yet more often than not, they are subtle, perhaps almost imperceptible at times. We must therefore cultivate an extremely attuned level of awareness in order to be able to recognize them. This chapter highlights three more significant concepts to help enhance this level of awareness, which will ultimately support us to clear a path forward for a more authentic relationship with our emotions.

To continue to relax further into fully experiencing our feelings, we must become even more deeply familiar with the following concepts:

- feeling instead of thinking
- deactivating intricate ego defense mechanisms
- the power of forgiveness.

Intimately understanding these key elements of repatterning our relationship with emotion will help us achieve new levels of personal growth and transformation.

THE MIND'S TRICKIEST BARRIER TO FEELING ...IS THINKING

Read that again!

This is a concept that most easily and most often slips by our awareness. Even those who really *understand* the realms of emotional growth and healing can, like everyone, become ensconced in thought without realizing it.

The critical thing to recognize here is that thinking about our emotions and our internal worlds is *not* the same as feeling them. Thinking about our emotions is just another ego protective defense mechanism, which, as we have explored in depth in this workbook, only serves to prevent us from fully feeling our feelings. To experience our emotions authentically and completely, as we know, requires that we *drop* our ego defense mechanisms, especially when it comes to thinking about our emotions rather than feeling them.

Most of us are intricately enmeshed with our own thoughts and place their value on an extremely high pedestal. But thoughts are nothing more than interpretations. We think they are true, and they may in fact be reflective of *our own* truth, but it is really just that—our own interpretation of reality. Recognizing this can allow us to take a step back from our thoughts, and from this slightly more objective space, we can start to let go of or even change those thoughts. As we did in one of our earlier skill-building exercises, when we step back and watch, we can then also ask: *Who is it who is doing the watching?*

Asking this question can lead us to an even deeper state of awareness. In fact, it can lead us to the recognition that all we really *are* is awareness, and when we fully recognize and embrace that, it can become a pure "aha" moment.

As you read through and do the experiential exercises in this chapter, and even as you continue on with your day, week, month, and year, you are invited to keep in mind the following perspectives: 1) All I am is awareness and 2) Every thought is just an interpretation.

Try also keeping these ideas in mind as you read through the following section, which identifies three primary ways that our protective ego mechanism often tries to keep us "safe" by shifting us into our thinking minds, rather than allowing us to relax fully into our emotions.

Three Ways the Mind Keeps Us Thinking Instead of Feeling

1. **Thinking about feeling.** Again, thinking about our feelings, and feeling our feelings, is not the same thing. In fact, these two acts use different parts of the brain and are actually mutually exclusive. Thinking about feelings is a survival and defense mechanism, while feeling our feelings is a release of these survival and defense mechanisms. Developing awareness of the difference between thinking about feeling and actually feeling helps us to know when we are truly allowing ourselves to feel an emotion, and when we are actually only thinking about that emotion.

2. **"I already know that."** This phrase, whether verbalized out loud, or said silently in one's own mind, may be one of the biggest ego defense mechanisms there is. When we believe that we already know something, it is most often the case that we truly only know a percentage of it. When we assume an inner posture of "I already know that," the important part is the energy that accompanies those words—these words most often possess a defensive charge, an indicator that we are holding unprocessed emotion. Sometimes this charge, especially when it is part of our inner posture rather than being verbalized out loud, can be very subtle and difficult to recognize, yet it nonetheless blocks us from truly feeling our feelings in that situation.

3. **Knowing truth versus living truth.** Often, we may think that we have made a *particular* truth part of our consciousness, when in reality, we only *know* that truth, *believe* in that truth, or *understand* that truth. This is very different from integrating and therefore *living* that truth, and this is especially important to be aware of when we are processing and integrating new truths about ourselves. We

may think that we have integrated new ways of being, when really, we have only *understood* them. In order to integrate them, we have to live them. We have to practice them. And importantly, we have to do so peacefully. If we are living a new truth but there is still a feeling of charge or intensity around it, it indicates that there is likely still something to work out and further integrate in that domain.

An important reminder here is that the goal in heightening our awareness about how our mind can sometimes keep us in a state of thinking rather than feeling is never to engage in self-criticism, but quite the contrary, to help us come closer to living in a more constant vibration of self-love and acceptance. In this state, energy is flowing, clear, and buoyant. Our goal is also not to live in a way in which we *never* get triggered or lose our footing, as that is a wholly unrealistic goal, but rather to achieve an anchor state of greater clarity and fewer triggers. This anchor state solidifies more and more as we continue to unblock our emotions. Our ultimate goal is always, essentially, to make more safe space for ourselves so that we can continue to process our feelings with self-love instead of fear.

Another important thing to note here is that sometimes, as we engage with our own personal processes of growth and transformation, and inevitably become aware of certain ego defense mechanisms, we must still be gentle with ourselves and listen to our own unique needs for timing. When we discover a particular ego defense mechanism at work, we might want to dismantle it right away, and while that may sometimes be the right thing to do, in other cases we might not be quite ready for that just yet.

So if you find on your journey that in a particular moment it does not feel like exactly the right time to dismantle the mechanism at hand, then that is okay as well. After all, this entire process is about self-compassion, and it is therefore compromised as soon as we begin to bully ourselves into change, or to push ourselves into feeling our feelings. We can never force ourselves or anyone else into feeling emotion, for one of the primary points we have explored throughout this workbook is that it is only *when we feel safe enough* to let down our patterned defenses, that new, healthier patterns will emerge.

That is why using the mantra, *it is safe to feel,* can be helpful. Whenever we are processing new ways of being and feeling, especially if it pertains to particularly difficult or uncomfortable emotions and situations, both past and present, we must approach ourselves with the utmost level of gentleness and care.

Identifying and Deactivating Ego Mechanisms

As we have continued to dissect and explore in this workbook, one of the key elements to shifting our relationship with our emotions is to deepen our level of awareness about ourselves.

Specifically, when we become more aware of the most subtle ways that our egos often try to protect us, yet which often instead take us further from feeling our true emotions, the more we are able to deactivate those mechanisms and soften even further into feeling our feelings.

Earlier in the workbook, we looked at a short list of "signals" that indicate to us when the ego may be erecting walls that block us from authentically engaging with our emotions. Here, we will look further at those mechanisms, as well as some others, and we will also practice an exercise for deactivating this guarded state once we become aware that it is present. Deactivating these ego mechanisms, when done with gentleness and self-compassion, can help us feel safe to release old modes of protection, and thus to more deeply relax into what we feel.

The key to deactivating these mechanisms is, first, to learn to identify them. It is only by bringing greater awareness to them that we can then do something to change them. In this way, awareness yields choice, and choice yields empowerment.

Here is a non-exhaustive list of easily recognizable ego protective mechanisms that we can practice learning to identify so that we can eventually deactivate them, thereby empowering ourselves instead to truly feel our emotions, and thus to transcend personal limitations on our path of self-growth and healing.

Repetitive thinking

When we notice ourselves reviewing something over and over again in the mind, this is often an indication that the mind is still trying effortfully to figure something out.

Repetitive storytelling

When we witness ourselves talk about the same thing repeatedly—for example, constantly telling the same story to multiple people—it usually means that there is an unprocessed emotion behind this story, one that likely cannot be navigated simply by repeating the story.

Withdrawal of expression

On the other hand, when we witness ourselves *not* talk about something that is important to us, while feeling in a state of either quiet desperation, isolation, or inability to say what we need, this is also an indication that we are not fully processing and feeling our emotions.

Autopilot /Disassociation

Sometimes we may become aware that we are participating in certain activities or behaviors while in a state of autopilot—we witness ourselves doing these things, know they are not in our best interest, yet continue to do them anyway. Some examples of this are: eating when not hungry, drinking too much, over-exercising, mindlessly shopping, etc. When we engage in these behaviors with a lack of awareness, we end up creating more blocks to feeling our underlying emotions.

It is important to note here that, very often, in the exact moments we identify and deactivate an ego mechanism, insights or massive shifts may not appear immediately. Instead, they often arrive later on when the mind is clear, when we are in a more fully relaxed state after processing our experiences; here, there is more space for integration, and for new thoughts and new ways of being to naturally emerge.

Sometimes, of course, there might be a "lightbulb moment" that brings with it instant realization and even integration, but in general, the process of deactivating our protective mechanisms is more akin to cleaning a room—it's not fun while we're doing it, but we feel the reward later when we re-enter the room, now so much cleaner and more peaceful than before.

This is important to understand so that our expectations are realistic, and we do not give the mind yet another reason to criticize or over-analyze our process of letting go. As mentioned in previous chapters, especially if we have been through a lot of challenges in our lives, and therefore have somewhat of a "thicker" story, then there will be more layers to dissolve. This calls for deeper self-compassion, more patience, and the understanding that, because there are a plethora of thoughts and beliefs embedded into our neurological networks, it typically takes time to rewire, and for new patterns of thoughts and insight to emerge.

Not only does this complex neurological network of thoughts and patterns mean that our process of changing our relationship to our emotions needs time to come fully to fruition, and for new ways of thinking and being to arise, it also means that as we start to make these shifts, we are in essence disturbing the network. Therefore, as this network begins to unravel, we can often at first experience greater levels of discomfort.

It is important to have this expectation that as we go through the process of opening up our feelings, we can sometimes feel like we are beginning to come "undone," in a sense. Without this awareness, we can often misinterpret this feeling to mean that we are regressing, when in fact it is actually an indicator that we are beginning to shift our old patterns, to take the lid off of all that we have been suppressing. In these moments, we may feel a greater calling for more emotional connection or support, or for more space and sacred solitude.

As highlighted in the last chapter, it is imperative to have a solid support person or network at your disposal as you begin to make these transformative shifts, so that if anything arises that feels beyond your ability to navigate on your own, you already have the proper supports in place to help you move forward on your path of personal growth.

BOX: PRACTICE & REFLECTION

Deactivation of Ego Protection

Create a space for yourself where you can sit peacefully and quietly. Begin this exercise with a few relaxing breaths. Allow yourself to become present with yourself as you sit and observe your internal environment and begin to watch your mind chatter. Are you playing a dialogue over and over in your chatter? Is there a storyline that you can not let go? Is there anything distracting you from being present in the moment? Simply stay curious about these aspects of your inner experience.

Since thinking and feeling cannot happen at the same time, ask yourself what is the sensation of the vibration of these thoughts? Do not focus on the actual words, focus gently on the vibration that the words are creating. Simply allow yourself to remain open and curious as you sit with the vibration of the sticky thoughts.

Your mind will naturally go back and forth between the story and the sensation but train your soft focus to rest on the sensation as you receive each sensation as just a sensation. Do not allow your mind to make a certain meaning out of the sensations; simply soften your body into them.

Without forcing or pushing, wait patiently until the vibrations soften and dissipate.

While in the process of this exercise, it is common that you may feel as though you are not doing it correctly. This experience is common with many of us during meditation.

However, every time you can shift your focus to the sensation and allow your body to process it, you are working toward your paradigm shift.

Your insights, clarity, and benefits will come after the practice is over.

NOTE: Begin this process with only sitting 10 to 15 minutes at a time. End your practice with three breaths.

DEPROGRAMMING GUILT AND SHAME

Throughout this workbook, we have explored the importance of getting comfortable with uncomfortable emotions, letting down our ego guard so that we can fully feel and process our feelings, and therefore move into new ways of being and living. We have also explored some specific tools for navigating this new, deeper relationship with ourselves.

If we wish to embrace ourselves fully, compassionately, and authentically, however, there is also one other critical step that we absolutely cannot skip. That step is: the dissolving of socially and culturally programmed guilt and shame about feeling and experiencing our emotions.

Guilt and shame are experiences that arise from *distorted perceptions* of ourselves, predominantly placed upon us either by social constructs, other people, or often, a combination of the two. It is extremely difficult to truly get to know ourselves, and to embrace everything we feel and experience in our internal worlds, if we feel guilty or ashamed about it. Therefore, in order to deepen our relationship with ourselves, and to evolve past old personal limitations, we have to learn to dissolve culturally or socially entrained feelings of guilt and shame that otherwise block us from deeper self-exploration, authentic connection, and personal transformation.

Take a moment to notice the use of the word *dissolve* here, rather than the more commonly used phrases, *to release* or *let go of.* This is intentional. There is a significant energetic difference when we think about the goal of *releasing* versus *dissolving.* Just as feeling our emotions is an *active* process, so is moving through our personal layers of guilt and shame.

Not only does it set an unrealistic goal to think of simply "releasing" these longstanding layers within ourselves, it also does not serve our growth. It is in the more active process of being with, understanding, learning from, and compassionately tending to our own feelings of guilt and shame that we much more effectively create an environment in which these layers that tend to block our growth can truly begin to peel away, or to dissolve.

In order to create the conditions for this to transpire, we must un-enmesh ourselves from the external sources that gave rise to these sensations of guilt and shame in the first place. Earlier, we discussed the concept of enmeshment as an over-identification with one's own emotions. Here, we can also understand it as a state of over-connectedness to other people's values, beliefs and feelings. This kind of enmeshment is completely normal, and we all experience it to some extent. In the early phases of development, we learn to mirror our caretakers' actions and behaviors in order to formulate an idea of how to be and function in the world. As we enter adolescence, we also begin to mirror our peers.

However, while some enmeshment with others is natural, it is its degree that determines whether or not we develop a healthy sense of self and individuality. And in turn, it is the level of our core sense of self that impacts our degree of happiness and contentment.

In order to dissolve guilt and shame, therefore, we must become aware of the difference between what has been unconsciously placed upon us by others and what we truly feel and believe in our own hearts. Once we begin to really examine our programming, we tend to realize more deeply that our feelings of guilt and shame are often stemming from a source outside of ourselves, usually a source that correlates to the guilt and shame of *others*.

That said, we of course maintain the power not to adopt these enmeshed feelings. Yet to individuate from enmeshed feelings is something that takes a significant amount of awareness and practice in order to come to know what we ourselves truly think, feel, and believe. It is then that we can energetically "give back" these projections to the source or person from which they originally came, dismantle our programming, and thereby actively dissolve our feelings of guilt and shame.

One of the most powerful reasons we continue to carry guilt and shame about feeling emotions is our culture's deeply rooted and collectively unconscious belief that if we experience emotions too deeply, especially more difficult emotions such as anger, fear, or sadness, it means that we are weak or broken, or that something is wrong with us.

More recently, this conversation has come to light specifically as it pertains to men and the lack of permission society affords them to feel and to express emotion. However, while it is certainly true that men experience a vast degree of societal programming in this way, every one of us, regardless of gender, learns through this cultural conditioning to suppress certain emotions. The types of emotion we are taught to suppress (e.g., typically sadness for men, or anger for women), do correspond to strong gender stereotypes, but nonetheless, at an early age, all of us become downloaded with this unhealthy and unbalanced approach to being in relationship with our emotions.

As we know, to experience emotion of any kind is simply to be human; and no matter how hard we may try, we cannot bypass this aspect of being human. When we try to do so, as we have explored, it greatly impacts both our physical and emotional wellbeing.

When it comes to feeling our feelings, an extremely important support for helping dissolve our programming around guilt and shame is to remember the *objective guiding principles* from Chapter 1, especially that all feelings are valid and are also simply records of the past. Every feeling just *is*. And the reason feelings just *are* is that they are simply physiological, neurological, and psychological records of our own personal history.

So often, we can feel ashamed of our emotions and equate them with weakness, instability, or inadequacy, but when we understand that everything we feel is completely normal given the past experiences that generated these visceral "records," we can take a step further in dissolving any guilt or shame we might experience about our emotions. As we practiced with the *3 N's* exercise in Chapter 2, we can come to recognize that anyone else who had experienced what we had would very likely feel much the same way.

Specifically, it is critical to keep in mind that as children, due to our less advanced stage of psychological and neurological development, we process life experience, as well as belief about ourselves and our core worth, through a lens of emotional interpretation rather than cognitive reasoning. We are therefore much more likely to interpret childhood experiences in ways that either create negative thoughts about ourselves, or build up ego defenses to keep our young psyches feeling safe.

Furthermore, not only do we generate certain patterns of thought and feeling when we interpret experiences through this developmentally-appropriate lens of perception, we also often internalize the patterns, thoughts, and emotions that were modeled for us by our parents, caregivers, and other family members. Because a family, as a unit, is always unconsciously seeking balance, there emerges in every family an unspoken system of emotional and energetic checks and balances, in which each of us (often unknowingly) assumes a role to help achieve that unconscious goal. Sometimes those roles can be positive and healthy, and other times, imbalances in energetic and psycho-socio-emotional familial dynamics can cause us to assume a personally disharmonious role that ends up impacting our beliefs about ourselves and our own emotions.

As we know, these early life experiences therefore set in motion a cycle of chemical reactions and resultant prewired feelings that tend to stay with us far into adulthood—that is, until we learn how to interrupt the cycle, and replace old beliefs with new ones. So many of our thoughts and feelings, and their corresponding neurological pathways, form at a very early age.

Therefore, our feelings do not have to make sense, nor are they anything for us to ever feel guilt or shame about, because they are merely a *record of the past*, a relic of when we processed life experience and belief about ourselves through a child's lens. When we are able to truly view our feelings simply as records of the past, and to understand the complex fabric of self and family that generated them, we can allow ourselves to objectively feel what we feel *without* guilt or shame. As adults, we now possess the cognitive capacity to compassionately acknowledge to that child within ourselves that there is nothing for us to feel guilty or ashamed about when it comes to feeling our emotions.

In fact, we can completely reverse our perception of what it means to experience emotion. While society may often give us the message, both directly and subconsciously, that to feel emotions is either a sign of weakness, or is "too much" and therefore burdensome to others, there is an alternative perspective that is now beginning to emerge in our culture.

This new lens illuminates that we are on the precipice of entering into a new way of being in the world and with each other, where traits such as emotional sensitivity, awareness, and authentic relationship with self and others will be considered strengths rather than weaknesses, and will in fact be paramount to successfully navigating this newly emerging social paradigm.

To withstand or "take" pain is not necessarily the powerful characteristic our culture often depicts it to be, as it is most often a trait that arises from misaligned old programming rooted in a *lack* of self-worth and self-compassion. As collective consciousness evolves, we are all standing at the edge of a paradigm shift that will see our ability to deeply feel our own emotions begin to emerge as one of the most powerful characteristics.

The moment we are able to fully surrender to our experience of emotion is the moment true acceptance emerges. And this acceptance is the initial seed of growth, power, and previously unfathomable change.

Susan Kullman

BOX: PRACTICE & REFLECTION

Deprogramming Guilt and Shame

In order to develop a healthy relationship with our emotions, and to help dissolve any guilt or shame that might be preventing us from truly feeling what we feel, it is important that we bring our awareness to the difference between present experience and old imprints from past stories and circumstances.

Also, recall that if there is high duration, frequency or intensity around certain past or present experiences, we will need to summon even greater compassion and space for ourselves to move through these feelings, and to feel safe enough to let down our ego defense mechanisms. Just as with anything else that requires rewiring of our nervous system, dissolving guilt and shame takes consistent practice—so if it takes a while for you to notice a change in the way you feel, this is completely normal and to be expected. The way we can cultivate trust in the process of dissolving guilt and shame, and in its profoundly positive impact on our wellbeing, is through practice, patience and consistency.

First, call to mind a situation where in hindsight you recognized your emotional reaction to the present situation was perhaps more intense than what seemed logical to you.

For example, maybe a friend arrived ten minutes late to meet you one time, and you felt either intense or long-lasting anger, anxiety, sadness, or any other emotion.

This is simply a moment for observation and nonjudgmental awareness of this emotional experience. Do your best to sit with yourself in silent witnessing as you become aware of these sensations.

Allow any mind chatter to drift into the background. The most important thing here is to hold yourself in the highest regard and compassion, and to allow your feelings to fully move through your body without any judgment whatsoever.

Next, you might try writing down answers to complete the following statements:

- The emotion(s) I felt during that situation were

  _____.

- A time I can remember seeing or hearing from someone or something else that it wasn't ok to feel (the emotion or emotions you wrote down above) was when _____.

If you'd like, you can also write down, or just say to yourself, the following:

- I realize now that any guilt or shame I might experience from feeling _____ has come from an external source that is not authentically who I am.

You might try repeating the mantra: *I am allowed to feel what I feel.*

Now would also be a great time to return to the 3 N's of Validation exercise box, applying the templates of inner dialogue provided there to the emotions that have arisen during this exercise.

Dissolving guilt and shame around feeling our emotions creates an opportunity for evolution to occur. Remain curious, open, and self-compassionate as your body processes the vibrations of your emotions.

After this exercise, write down any reflections or insights that might have arisen.

THE POWER OF FORGIVENESS

In general, the primary key to softening into feeling our feelings is to shift from a vibration of fear to a vibration of love. One of the most powerful ways that we can achieve this significant shift is through the process of forgiveness.

Forgiveness, in this sense, never equates to condoning a perpetrator's actions, nor does it mean that we even have to continue any kind of relationship with a person whose words or actions we feel have been harmful to us. Instead, true forgiveness is a shift in one's own state of mind, an authentic form of self-protection and healing, as it allows for the forgiver's ultimate release of any toxic energy that may have accumulated due to experiences in the relationship.

When we continue to carry toxic energy with us, which we often do for very long periods of time—sometimes years, or even an entire lifetime—we unknowingly bring it with us into every part of our lives, where it then takes up valuable space in the mind, heart, and body. This contamination itself causes us continual harm, on top of what may have already been inflicted by the other person's behavior.

This is such an important distinction to remember when it comes to understanding forgiveness, and the value it possesses in our own process of reorganizing our relationship to ourselves and our emotions—in other words, the value it has in our own healing. Often, we hold onto grudges either due to feelings of self-righteousness, or simply because of our pain and a lack of tools for learning to dissolve it, but when we hold onto this pain, we render ourselves prisoners of past situations. We continue to relive them in our minds, and every time we do that, we unintentionally strengthen the corresponding neurological connections and pathways, which then produce results in the body that mirror the old situation, exactly as if it had happened yesterday. And these feelings, in turn, continue to cyclically produce the same stories, thoughts, emotions, cellular chemical imprints, words and behaviors.

To elaborate more specifically, since our thoughts greatly contribute to generating our choices and behaviors in the world, the neurological reinforcement that arises when we do not practice forgiveness can often lead us to *participate* in similar situations in the future, rather than drawing new boundaries and thus creating healthier situations and relationships. In this way, through a lack of forgiveness, we can do unintentional harm to ourselves by inhibiting our own growth and reinforcing old patterns of choice and behavior in new situations.

On the other hand, when we are able to proactively practice forgiveness in any situation through a lens of self-healing, by relaxing into the emotions that may be uncomfortable so that they have the space to fully pass through us, we can free ourselves from the vibrational charge of the story around that situation. Furthermore, we also become much more likely to change the story of our future relationships through a new set of choices and behaviors that honor ourselves in a deeper, more authentic way. Forgiveness is therefore not something we do for another person; it is something we do to honor ourselves, and to set ourselves free.

Another pivotal aspect of forgiveness in the process of reforging a healthy relationship with ourselves and our emotions is *self-forgiveness*. So often, we hold grudges against ourselves, or unnecessarily carry shame, for many different things. But we can reframe the parts of ourselves that need work instead of blaming ourselves for them, and we have already explored some ways to do that—such as offering ourselves acknowledgement, validation, and compassion, as well as bringing greater cognitive understanding to how our past experiences and neurophysiological development may have contributed to shaping certain aspects of who we have become in our present lives.

In fact, when we do this—truly bringing compassion to ourselves and our perceived limitations—what we most often find is that there is actually nothing at all to forgive. Most often, we are simply in need of greater levels of love, validation, and acknowledgement. And while we might desire to receive these things from others, and it may in fact be possible, it is most important that we are able first to give them to ourselves.

In reframing our present challenges, it can also be helpful to embrace the concept that every one of us has a "dark" side, and that this is true for every single human being on the planet. Just like the ego, what we commonly refer to as a dark side, contrary to how it is often discussed, is in fact not "bad"; rather, it simply refers to the parts of ourselves that we have *labeled* and *judged* as bad or undesirable, and have therefore suppressed, denied our own love, and have literally relegated to the darkness—a place beyond our conscious awareness. At any time, however, we can choose to bring these parts of ourselves back into view, to give them the love they really need, and therefore to dissolve any uncomfortable emotions that these parts may carry.

It is therefore neither necessary nor helpful to hide this side of ourselves; rather, the complete opposite is true. Authentic healing and transformation at the deepest levels actually *requires* us to embrace every part of ourselves, and to realize and integrate that there is no shame in any of these parts. We all have limitations, insecurities, and areas of pain, learning, and potential growth. For all of us, though, our greatest limitations arise when we fail to embrace these parts of ourselves.

It is quite easy, after all, to embrace our strengths and positive attributes, and to feel love for and confidence in ourselves as a result. But when we also embrace these sometimes more difficult or seemingly less desirable parts of ourselves, it is then that our true power arises, for in fully embracing all of who we are, we can come to see that there is nothing left to fear.

We can reach an elevated state of unconditional self-acceptance and self-compassion, notice and offer love to those parts of ourselves we would like to shift, and most importantly, release self-judgment. This self-judgment most often stems from our early programming and what was modeled for us during early life—whether we experienced judgment placed on us, or even just saw people around us judging and not fully embracing themselves with compassion and awareness.

We can practice releasing this programmed tendency toward self-judgment by continually bringing awareness to the reminder that any parts of us we may judge negatively are arising *only* because they are calling our attention to the need for greater levels of self-love and self-acceptance.

And the more we practice this heightened level of self-forgiveness, the easier it becomes to also forgive others, which is, again, an act that is always for our own growth and healing.

BOX: PRACTICE & REFLECTION

Forgiveness

Before beginning the following exercise in forgiveness, remember that forgiveness does *not* mean that you are condoning or in alignment with others' potentially harmful words or actions, nor does it suggest in any way that you must restore relationships with anyone who has harmed you or trespassed your boundaries.

The intention of this exercise is to invite you to begin the process of moving through the often tension-filled energy that we tend to carry in our bodies when holding grudges or resentments. It is deliberately designed to help you care for your entire being by allowing your body to sense, feel, and move through these places of tension, gripping and holding.

Begin by thinking of one thing for which you have not forgiven either someone else or yourself.

Write down this one thing in your journal. Let your pen freely express everything that you have been keeping inside or repressing about it. Be *completely* open about what you feel. Remember that these words are for your eyes only, so feel free to express yourself without inhibition.

When you have finished writing all of your thoughts and feelings about this one thing, complete your writing by adding the following phrase at the end:

"... and anything else that I may have forgotten to write down at this moment."

Next, create a sacred space to prepare a short ceremony that will acknowledge your intention of forgiveness for this person or for yourself.

In a safe place, and using a flame-resistant container, burn the piece of paper that contains your thoughts and feelings about this topic. As the paper is dissolving, imagine that you are witnessing yourself transcending all resentment and tension around this particular situation or set of feelings. Repeat to yourself (either silently or aloud) an intention of release and forgiveness from deep within the heart of your inner witness, or from any part of yourself that feels a strong desire for emotional freedom.

Acknowledging your own emotions, and setting the intention of forgiveness through this act of self-compassion, will begin a process of gentle unwinding throughout your entire being. It may take some time to completely unravel all the layers of the old holding vibration as your ego starts to feel safe enough to reveal and release each one. Every time this vibration of tension or holding arises, treat it as an opportunity to sense, feel and relax further into it, and thereby, to release it.

Do your best to move through any discomfort with patience and self-acceptance, knowing that if these emotions are presenting themselves, it is because they are ready to process through you completely, and then to dissolve. Also remember that this is deep work you are doing, even if it may seem simple on the surface, so be sure to practice gentleness with yourself before, during, and after this exercise.

Also, note that to feel a heightening of uncomfortable emotions during this process is completely normal, and in fact indicates that you are making progress and moving closer to an energetic state of forgiveness, as each layer of emotion arises, and then peels away. The only thing you need to do is to stay with this process by continuing to deeply relax into any discomfort that may arise. Remember to call on your inner witness (as well as your support network, should you feel you need it) in order to do so.

Susan Kullman

Susan Kullman

CHAPTER SIX

NEUROSCIENCE AND NON-JUDGMENT

*"Every aspect of thought and emotion
is rooted in brain structure and function..."*

- STEVEN PINKER

Susan Kullman

WE HAVE THUS FAR EXPLORED various ways to enhance our awareness and release self-judgment in the transformation of our relationship to our emotions and to ourselves.

Another way we can cultivate greater self-awareness and non-judgment is to further our understanding of neuroscience. Sometimes, increasing our comprehension about the way our brains work with regard to our emotions helps to place a little more space between us and our experiences of those emotions.

While we of course want to be careful not to overanalyze, or to mistake thinking about our emotions for actually feeling them—which, as we know, are two common ego protective mechanisms that take us *further* from feeling our feelings—sometimes gaining insight into the behavioral science behind our emotions can help us become more objective about them. And if we can harness this objectivity to allow ourselves to more fully experience our emotions without fear and judgment, then we can use this enhanced intellectual understanding to actually deepen our relationship to our emotions.

WHY NON-JUDGMENT IS CRITICAL
TO PERSONAL CHANGE

As we have discussed, one of the primary contributors to suppressing our awareness of old, non-serving patterns, is self-judgment. When there is a part of ourselves that we do not like, or wish were different, rather than bringing that part to light and offering ourselves the love, kindness, and gentleness we need to shift that aspect of who we are, we often instead choose to judge or criticize ourselves. And because that self-judgment is so painful, doing so commences a cycle of then pushing those parts of ourselves even further away so that we do not have to experience the self-criticism that arises along with them. Yet because these parts of ourselves, and their accompanying emotions, can never be permanently released without first being fully acknowledged and experienced, attempting to do so only leads to blockage, imbalance, unrest, and even disease in the mind and body.

What is interesting to note, though, is that when we attempt to push these parts of ourselves away, what we are truly pushing away is not actually the part or emotion itself, but the pain that arises from our own self-judgment and self-criticism of that part of ourselves.

Therefore, If we desire to evolve and to create new experiences in body and mind, and therefore in our lives in general, we must become more objective and non-judgmental about our emotions so that we feel safer to fully experience them.

We so often judge our feelings, our thoughts, our bodies, and ourselves in general, and in these self-judgments we tend to be extremely harsh. So it's no wonder that we then often do not feel safe enough to fully experience our emotions and all of who we are; if we wish to create that space of internal safety, practicing non-judgment with ourselves is the key. Often, we might even believe that we are not judging ourselves, and yet our self-judgment may have become such a familiar internal state of being and thinking that we may not even recognize when we are in it—self-judgment might come to feel neutral, when in fact it is self-critical.

It is important to remember that self-judgment serves in no way to help us. To be discerning, responsible, integrity-oriented, compassionate people, we of course need to engage in *self-reflection*, but when our goal is to evolve past our previous boundaries and limitations, self-judgment is, at worst, detrimental, and at best, unhelpful. In fact, the minute we begin to judge ourselves, all progression and personal evolution comes to a halt.

This is because, when we judge ourselves, we instantly create a limiting belief. And furthermore, as soon as we judge anything at all—partners, friends, situations, or anything else—we subconsciously label it as something negative, and thus begin to form in the brain a neural association that may eventually become an even more intricately wired belief system. Once this happens, it becomes ever more challenging to alter this wired network of associations and beliefs—it is absolutely still *possible*, as we will soon explore, yet it makes our lives a lot easier if we practice awareness and non-judgment as we go. This more even progression helps to dissolve the unhelpful neurological connections in smaller increments, or even sometimes to prevent them from forming in the first place, rather than to unravel an already wired system of emotion, thought, story, words, and actions.

The neural network of self-judgment is one that many of us have "grooved" very well, because we have unconsciously practiced over and over again what was modeled for us, or what we interpreted situations to mean about ourselves, during our early lives. And as we know, every time we practice this cycle, we create an even more deeply grooved network, activating and strengthening its neurological pathways, and making it more difficult to deconstruct. Nevertheless, it *is* possible to deconstruct a neurological pathway or network.

Essentially, this amounts to breaking either a physical or emotional addiction. An addiction is simply something—whether a physical activity, external substance, or our own thoughts or emotions—that produces a chemically wired response in the brain, and a subsequently well-grooved network of neural pathways. To break any kind of addiction, therefore, we must learn to rewire these networks. And when it comes to our emotions in particular, the way to do this is primarily through the practice of self-awareness and non-judgment.

When we are able to be completely honest with ourselves and acknowledge what we truly feel and experience within, rather than solely what we present to the external world, that is when we are mostly likely to be able to experience and create change in our own lives, and also in the world around us. When we find a way to lessen self-judgment, and replace it instead with self-compassion and understanding, we no longer feel the same need to push certain parts of ourselves or our emotions into the periphery, and can instead acknowledge them with greater awareness and self-compassion. In doing so, we initiate the generation of an entirely new neurological network, and thus a corresponding cycle of growth and transformation.

BOX: PRACTICE & REFLECTION

Objectivity and Self-Compassion

Given that objectivity and non-judgment is such a critical key to developing greater self-compassion and a greater capacity for healing and personal growth, it is important to ask yourself the following question:

How can I become more objective and self-compassionate about my programming, my emotions, and how I show up in the world?

Again, when it comes to our feelings, harnessing the intellectual knowledge about how our neurological patterning leads to our emotional responses can allow us more space to simply observe— to "look and see what's there" rather than labeling our emotions and experiences as positive or negative, "shoulds" or "shouldn'ts", or with any judgmental words at all.

A simple way to heighten our objectivity about our emotions or experiences is to meet them with the inner witness, by practicing internally responding to any rising emotion with neutral yet genuine phrases such as: "Isn't that interesting?" or "Oh, look at that..."

To say these words to ourselves in the absence of any judgment, but instead with an open, curious, and compassionate heart, is a great way to begin to open new doors to understanding, and to be able to more fully experience our deepest and sometimes most difficult emotions.

Take a moment to reflect on and write down some thoughts in response to the following question:

Given the fact that emotions are neurological patterns, what could you identify as a well-grooved pattern that you often experience? For example, if you reflect on your typical internal state of being, would you say that you most often have an inner experience of frustration, sadness, anxiety, a general sense of mistrust, a feeling of too much or too little energy, or perhaps even joy, excitement, awe, or inspiration? We so often tend to assign our emotional responses to different things, places, events, or people; however, if you simply look at your emotional responses as an internally well-grooved pattern, what new aspects of them do you see? How does this potentially change the way you might think about them, and about yourself?

When we remove all the individual reasons and stories we assign to our emotions, we can begin to see a pattern emerge. This is the pattern that is imprinted in the pathways of the brain. When we practice responding to these patterns with the objectivity of the inner witness, we can heighten our ability for nonjudgmental awareness and reflection, and strengthen our muscles of self-validation.

Now, try completing the following phrase to the best of your ability, and write down your answers to the questions that follow:

- Given how, when, and by whom I was raised, it is normal that my brain developed this pattern because…..

- Do you feel that any tendencies towards self-judgment have yielded positive results in the realm of your personal growth thus far?

- How might you use the preliminary understanding of the neuroscience of emotions presented here to help you more often turn to self-reflection instead of self-judgment? How might it even help you to release any shame you might feel about experiencing your emotions, and encourage you instead to bring greater self-compassion to your continuing process of internal evolution, awareness and personal transformation?

While breaking the chains of any habit or pattern may not always seem valuable in the beginning (since, as you may recall, that is the well-intentioned yet misguided attempt of your ego mind to try to protect you by keeping you in the same familiar place), you might be surprised at the effectiveness of this seemingly simple process of practice and reflection, and its ability to aid your movement into greater nonjudgmental awareness of yourself and your emotions.

BREAKING FREE FROM THE
UNCOMFORTABLE COMFORT ZONE

As we have just learned, experiences in life can create certain feelings and associations in our brain, and if we lose awareness of our own power to change these patterns, we can end up continuously repeating them. A recent study from psychologists at Queen's University in Kingston, Ontario and published in the journal Nature Communications, says that the average human has 6,200 thoughts per day. (Tseng, J., Poppenk, J. "Brain meta-state transitions demarcate thoughts across task contexts exposing the mental noise of trait neuroticism." Nature Communication, 11, 3480, July 2020.)

This is a pretty powerful statistic, especially when we consider that our thoughts create our choices, which then create our behaviors, which then create our experiences, which then create our emotions, which then tend to *recreate* the same original thought that began the cycle. We can see, therefore, that it can be relatively easy to become stuck in a circuit of thought and emotion.

It is this neurologically wired circuit that dictates our habits. Habits might include things we do when we get up in the morning, when we get to work or our destination for the day, when we go to sleep, and everything in between. The routines we have, such as what side of the bed we get up on, the way we brush our teeth, how we have our coffee, and the time we walk the dog, are all manifestations of grooved neurological pathways that tend to yield very similar experiences each day.

As long as we continue to allow the brain to work in the same way every day, we will repeatedly create the same reality. There may be minor variations, of course, but in general, we become entrenched in the habits that make us feel safe and in control of what is happening. This does not mean that we *are* actually in control—and in fact, often, we are even less in control when our subconscious patterns are playing out without our greater awareness—but our habits still make us *feel* like we are in control, and that feeling is something we tend to crave.

This is because change can be challenging for our nervous systems.

This does not need to be the case, but unless we have deliberately practiced opening to change, and programming ourselves to feel safe doing so, most of us have a tendency to remain bound to predictable patterns of behavior.

The key element to understand here is that, not only do we engage in these predictable patterns and give them preference over change, but interestingly, we also tend to remain in these patterns *even when they are no longer working in our best interest.*

This, of course, is usually not a conscious choice we make. In fact, it is more akin to an *absence* of conscious choice that allows the underlying neural mechanisms informing our behavior and emotions to continue to operate below the level of our consciousness. Until we make these patterns conscious and use our own power to create and embrace change, we remain bound to old and often non-serving circuits of behavior. This is what we might call *the uncomfortable comfort zone.*

So how does the idea of the uncomfortable comfort zone relate to emotions?

As stated earlier, we all have an addiction to certain emotions. We are addicted to these feelings and emotions because of habit, and we therefore tend to experience them in repeating cycles. As a result, we also subconsciously generate experiences and relationships that constantly recreate those emotions so that they fulfill and affirm our expectations about who we think we are, because this feels familiar and comfortable for us at many levels.

This is an essential aspect of the idea of comfort zones—that our nervous systems are wired for the preference that we always continue to feel "like ourselves," and their resultant natural trajectory therefore aims to keep us in a state of stasis.

In other words, we tend to create comfort zones of identity. The particular identities we create for ourselves, which include all of our thoughts, emotions, experiences and relationships, ensure that we continue to create the same "comfortable" or familiar belief systems, emotions, states of being, and experiences.

Notice the difference between the connotations of the words

comfortable and *familiar*. Even though we refer to our ingrained habits, ways of being, emotions, and identities as *comfort zones*, remember that often what we experience within our comfort zones is in fact not truly comfortable or desirable at all! While this is therefore neither functional nor logical when it comes to improving our emotional states and our general wellbeing, it is nevertheless what we are biologically programmed to do.

Until, that is, we change the program.

So how do we do that? When it comes to changing this program, it is critical to take a step back, to really observe our own patterns, and to notice how they show up in our life experiences and relationships. Furthermore, understanding how these patterns might first come to be can help us to become more objective and neutral rather than to judge ourselves for them, which then opens the door of possibility to change.

As a reminder, these patterns we all create and become accustomed to almost always develop due to a particular experience or set of experiences during childhood. And since as children our brains had not yet developed certain critical functions, any experience we had was filtered through a lens of emotional perception rather than rational analysis and comprehension. Because our emotions are records of the past, even though as adults we may intellectualize a story so that we understand it in a functional and mature way, this does not necessarily change the way we feel it in the body; these emotions become stored in physiological memory.

Furthermore, as children, our brain waves are also slower. They contain mostly delta waves, which are slower than the waves characteristic of a more mature brain. As delta waves convert to higher frequency waves such as beta waves, we are more able to process experiences through a lens of intellectual understanding and reflection. When we are young, though, and our brain waves are moving more slowly, we are much more permeable and susceptible to being emotionally impacted even by small or seemingly trivial experiences we may encounter. Whenever we witness and then interpret something, it "sticks," and it becomes a deep, intricately woven part of the fabric of who we are. This is why it can take some patient unraveling to shift these old perceptions about ourselves and our experiences.

To be more specific, because as children we interpret events without the use of fully matured deductive reasoning and executive functioning skills, we will always make an experience mean something about ourselves—perhaps that we are bad, unloveable, not good enough, etc. We have to think this way because, evolutionarily, children cannot think of their parents, from whom they seek fulfillment of survival-based needs, as bad. In fact, it is not until later childhood that we even process the concept of separation between ourselves and our parents, or ourselves and the world. Until then, it is extremely challenging for a child to conceptualize a parent as being bad or wrong, and he or she will therefore strongly attach to everything the parent says and does. Therefore, whatever was modeled for us as children becomes what we learn, and the experiences that we had (and our interpretations of them) become deeply wired into our neurological pathways of emotion and behavior.

When we become objective about our patterned emotions and experiences by deeply understanding their complex origin, and furthermore, when this new state of healthy objectivity and understanding helps yield the kind of gentle self-validation and self-compassion we have explored in depth throughout this workbook, we can then foster a more authentic relationship with whatever the emotion or pattern may be, and as a result, it actually loses its power over us; it changes.

When we begin to undo old perceptions, modern neuroscience has shown that because of a powerful characteristic of the human brain called *neuroplasticity*, it is extremely possible to rewire our neural networks. Neuroplasticity refers to the brain's ability to undergo change, even during adulthood, in order to compensate for lost neural networks by forming new ones. We can actually harness this fluid quality of the brain to break old addictions, whether physical or emotional, and to forge new, healthier neural pathways that in turn create a different set of emotions, thoughts, behaviors, and ultimately, experiences.

This is an extremely hopeful idea—one that didn't exist until fairly recently. At one time, behavioral scientists believed that our entire personalities were more or less determined and hardwired by the time we reached a relatively early period of adulthood. Now, however, it is understood that this is actually not the case, and that in fact, our brains can still change at any age. It follows, then, that there is also no time limit for changing our relationship to our emotions and experiences, and that therefore, we can also—*at any age*—surpass our former limitations.

We can thus harness realistic optimism as we set out to do this extremely important work of inner transformation, knowing that it is an endeavor rooted in the science of human change and growth, and that regardless of age or past experience, this change (even at the level of our neurophysiology) is absolutely possible.

BOX: PRACTICE & REFLECTION

Breaking free of your Uncomfortable Comfort Zone

As we have explored, the first step in making any shift in our internal environment is to heighten our awareness.

The same is true when it comes to breaking free of your own "uncomfortable comfort zone". Try some of the following practices to help with this shift:

- Take a moment to step back and become a witness to your general mood or internal vibration. What does it feel like? Is it familiar to you? You might notice yourself thinking things like, *This is just who I am*, or *This is how I feel all the time*. Even if you are feeling a distinct or more intense emotion in the current moment, do you recognize this feeling, or way of feeling, as something you have experienced before?

Pause here and write some reflections on either the familiarity or distinctness of your current mood, vibration, or emotion.

- Next, close your eyes briefly and think about the notion that although your current general mood or vibration may feel like who you are because it has so often been your internal experience and orientation to life, it is perhaps not *who* you are. Rather, it may be just one aspect of an identity that you have come to associate with over time.

And since our moods, vibrations, thoughts, and emotions generate our patterns of behavior, it is therefore also vital to recognize that just as you, as an entire being, are not solely these internal states, you are also not solely your external behavior. Behavior is, after all, simply a series of actions. And actions can change. You are much more than your internal states, and you are much more than your external behavioral patterns.

- Now, having reflected on that idea, gently call to mind an area in your life where some of your behavioral patterns may have caused you pain and discomfort, and do your best to write down answers to the following questions:

Can you identify some of the difficult thoughts or the emotions you may still hold when it comes to your pain and discomfort in this area?

Can you identify any repeating thoughts you might have about these behavioral patterns, and even perhaps why you feel your pain and discomfort with these patterns might be unchangeable—perhaps thoughts such as, That is just who I am, for example?

Write down a few of these repeating thoughts, if any come to you.

- Take a look at the thoughts and emotions you have written down, and see if you can start to identify any particular pattern(s) of belief. Ask yourself and write down answers to the following questions:

Do you think these patterns are yours alone, or might they have been passed down through multiple generations and cultures within your familial system?

Were these beliefs formed when you were a young, dependent child, and therefore the result of a young mind's interpretation of life experiences?

Were these beliefs possibly a result of someone else's interpretations that you unconsciously and unknowingly adopted as your own?

What do you think might have transpired differently in terms of your currently developed beliefs, thoughts, emotions, and behaviors had you grown up in a different home or environment? What patterns might you have acquired instead?

How might you begin to slowly adapt your current belief patterns about who you are and what you experience within, as well as what you do, in order to create both the internal states and external experiences you most desire?

As you feel into shifting some of these belief patterns towards new ones that serve you more fully and allow you to fulfill your highest potential, you might experience an internal resistance or a feeling that you will "never be able to" change your patterning and experience.

This resistance or doubt is actually where the important work of deep shifting truly begins, as it is one of the primary barriers that stands between each one of us and our highest potentials. To harness it for the most transformative outcome, do your best to just be with any doubt, discomfort or resistance that arises, and most importantly, as we have practiced many times throughout this workbook, *relax into it from a place of awareness and without judgment.*

Sit compassionately with all of your arising emotions and internal sensations until they dissipate and dissolve. As mentioned earlier in the book, these layers of long-buried vibrations and emotions will not necessarily disappear immediately. The duration, frequency and intensity of how long, how often, and how intensely these internal sensations have existed for you, will determine how much love, patience, and compassion you will need to bring to yourself and what you have experienced.

It is extremely important also to remember that we can, and must, bring compassion and love to ourselves with a sense of empowerment rather than victimization. This is where objectivity becomes paramount. The more you practice this, the greater degree of objectivity you will develop, until you eventually become both objective *and* compassionate at the same time. This is the cultivation of both self-love and self-empowerment simultaneously, which is a potent key to transformational healing and self-growth.

It is from this place that true change begins to transpire, and unlimited possibilities fall within reach. The degree to which you are able to bring these new possibilities to fruition is symbiotically dependent on how vulnerable you are willing to become, and how courageously you are willing to dismantle your inner walls. For while these walls aim understandably to protect you, they so often end up instead guarding the gates to your greatest treasures and to your highest potential. Taking even small or seemingly imperceptible steps to break free of your own uncomfortable comfort zone, will yield the key to unlock those gates, and to create the wellbeing you both desire and deserve.

USING NEUROSCIENCE TO TRANSCEND OUR BIGGEST OBSTACLE TO CHANGE

In the process of repatterning our emotions and their corresponding neural networks, blame is one obstacle that often presents the largest challenge for many people.

The tendency to blame others is something that we all possess to varying degrees. The reason is that, as we touched upon earlier, blame is an ego protective mechanism, and it is one that is extremely tempting to engage.

What does blame "protect" us from? Simply put, blame "protects" us from owning what we really feel. This, however, is not *true* protection. In fact, it is actively harmful to our relationship with ourselves, and specifically, to our relationship with our own emotions, as it blocks us from that key aspect of our journey of self-transformation—fully and authentically feeling our feelings.

In order to understand how blame blocks us from feeling our true emotions, it is important to know one thing: when we feel angry or sad (or any other emotion) at another person's words or actions, it is actually not that person's behavior that is truly causing us to feel that way. We feel the way we do because, as we have explored, those emotions are already *pre-wired* in our minds and bodies.

We are therefore primed to feel these emotions even before anyone says or does anything at all. In our present day lives, other people's behavior then merely serves as a *trigger* for those harbored and prewired emotions to rise to the surface.

To be clear, as mentioned in the section of this workbook about forgiveness, this does not mean that if someone says or does something hurtful or harmful, that we condone or excuse those words or actions, or that we even continue a relationship with that person; it means, simply, that we recognize that our own emotional wiring can often render our present moment reactions disproportionate to the actual events that are transpiring.

Perhaps, for example, frustration is one of the emotions we are addicted to, and in one instance we find a friend's words to be so frustrating that it prevents us from sleeping for three nights in a row. This may be an indication that the frustration we feel, while perhaps initiated by that friend's genuine lack of sensitive communication skills, is likely also a manifestation of long-harbored and strongly wired emotional pathways in the mind and body—ones that probably stem from childhood, and require nonjudgmental observation in order to shift.

Recognizing and integrating the recognition that *all* emotions we feel, even when triggered by the words and actions of others, are uniquely and utterly our own, is both the most significant challenge and the most important catalyst in the process of self-transformation. This is because it is one of the most direct pathways to truly feeling our emotions. Viewing our responses and reactions in this light helps keep this work an "inside job," and while that means that we are completely responsible for (not *guilty* for, but *responsible* for), all of our emotions, it also means that no one else wields any power over our experience greater than that which we wield ourselves.

Owning this, however, is no easy task, as we have been so conditioned to avoid the depths of our feelings, and instead to use powerful ego protective mechanisms like blame to divert the intensity of our emotions to external sources. It is natural, therefore, that we may feel resistance to the process of shifting that unconscious tendency. We might even feel resistance to the very idea that our emotions are arising from these well-grooved neural pathways, which are merely "turned on" by external situations, people, experiences, etc.—but which already existed, ready to be turned on in the first place.

Just as with everything else we feel, whenever we experience a sense of resistance, the best way to move through it is to be with it. To allow it to be there, to feel it fully, and to offer ourselves non-judgment, compassion, and validation so that whatever part of us is creating that resistance feels safe enough to let go, and therefore to surmount that block to growth and healing.

To recap, non-judgment and self-compassion are integral to self-growth and transformation, and understanding the neuroscience of our emotions can help provide us with the cognitive space and objectivity that precede these states of internal safety. When our internal environment becomes safer, we in turn feel more able to fully experience our emotions, and therefore, to move beyond them.

The bottom line is this: we have options. By coming to understand our own inner landscapes from multiple new angles, we provide ourselves with the gift of opening to novel possibilities. No matter how long we have a felt a certain way, or how many times different situations have caused us to feel the same thing (because, as we now know, it is prewired in us to feel that way), we do not have to continue to feel the same way, to think the same thoughts, or to create the same realities day after day.

We have choices, and we have the power to change our choices. Furthermore, our greatest power comes from fully owning what we feel, being with it compassionately no matter how uncomfortable it may be, and allowing it to move through us in all its intensity. This is very different than experiencing our emotions from a place of personal enmeshment, a state in which we believe that we *are* our emotions, which therefore makes it very difficult to gain enough space so that we can view them objectively and compassionately. Understanding how all human brains work when it comes to the realm of emotions can help begin to disentangle us from that web of enmeshment so that we can feel safe to actually experience our emotions.

The second critical thing to keep in mind on this journey of healing and self-transformation is that when we wish to evolve and create the life we desire, we have to authentically integrate the understanding that *our internal environments create our external environments*. Not the reverse. As humans, we often believe, due to our unconscious programming and protective mechanisms, that we will be happy when... something external happens.

In fact, though, the opposite is actually true; when we change our internal experience so that we are able to more often organically feel vibrations such as abundance, inspiration, joy, and gratitude, for example, it is then, and only then, through the literal rewiring of our neural networks responsible for thought, emotion, behavior and resulting experience, that we begin to see situations and people show up in our external world to match and recreate these new vibrations. This is how we harness non-judgment, self-compassion, and neuroplasticity for positive personal life change. In the next chapter, we will further explore these *life-giving* vibrations, and how to cultivate them authentically from within.

BOX: PRACTICE AND REFLECTION

Using Neuroscience to Transcend Our Biggest Obstacle to Change

- Think about one or two emotions that you feel you may have become addicted to throughout the course of your life. What is your experience with these emotions? If you try not to blame any external event for these emotions, and instead look at them as a result of certain neurological pathways that began forming at a young age, what do you witness? How does this feel to you?

- What thoughts do you witness yourself thinking when you are experiencing any of your addictive emotions?

- How do you witness yourself acting when you are experiencing that group of emotions and their accompanying sensations? What are your precipitating behaviors or habits? What neurologically wired emotional pattern do you imagine you might be playing out here?

- What do you notice about how the addictive thought and feeling cycle may have created certain aspects of your current identity? And how might this identity differ from your deeper, more authentic core self—the one that naturally exists beyond the level of neurologically wired emotional patterns?

Susan Kullman

Susan Kullman

CHAPTER SEVEN

FEELING OUR WAY TO JOY AND RADICAL SELF-TRANSFORMATION

"The joy we feel has little to do with the circumstances of our lives, and everything to do with the focus of our lives. "

- RUSSEL M. NELSON

Susan Kullman

PERPAPS BY THIS POINT IN the workbook, you have already encountered some experiential glimpses into the deeper transformative potential of cultivating a more authentic and vulnerable relationship with your own emotions. Or perhaps you are still wondering about the larger purpose of this work: how is it significant, and where can it ultimately lead?

A key notion to understand when exploring the answer to these questions is that, in the very same way we once became conditioned to uncomfortable emotions such as grief, frustration, and anger, we can also become conditioned to the experiences of joy and fulfillment.

Furthermore, it is the exact same practice of softening into our *uncomfortable* emotions that will simultaneously allow us also to open ourselves further to joy; this is true because the same walls that "protect" us from feeling uncomfortable feelings, also block the emotions we most desire to feel, like love and joy.

When we dismantle these walls, our ensuing openness is universal across all emotions, both the uncomfortable and the desirable. And since our internal states generate thoughts and behaviors, which generate corresponding realities, this softening into our own emotions also allows us eventually to create the life experiences that we truly desire.

In the *Wizard of Oz*, right before returning home, Dorothy exclaims that the scarecrow—with his brainless purity and innocence—is the one she will likely miss the most. As adults, one of the most healing salves for our overactive minds is the occasional return to a child-like, nonintellectual way of being. This is because, while intellect can be a wonderful tool in navigating our way through the world, at a certain threshold, our thinking minds (read: a potential defense mechanism of the ego) start to usurp energy that would otherwise go towards simply feeling and being present.

Another challenge that the thinking mind poses to our self-growth and transformation is its uncanny ability to successfully convince us that we always need a reason—usually in the form of some kind of logical storyline—in order to justify feelings like joy and gratitude. When we connect more directly to the heart, however, just as a child (or a brain-less scarecrow) might, it is then that we can experience joy and gratitude beyond reason, unattached to any particular story or thought.

And when we cultivate this practice, we develop the skill of being able to tap into our own joy at *any* moment, regardless of what is happening in the external world—joy becomes a state generated from within, independent of circumstance. This frees us immeasurably, for now we can genuinely *create* our joy, rather than seek it. And the empowerment that this affords us is invaluable, for it means that we have become the creators of our own realities in a way that is neither magic nor mysticism, but rather the tangible result of cultivating a more vulnerable and open relationship with our own emotions.

LETTING DOWN THE GRATITUDE GUARD: THE SANCTITY OF EVERYDAY LIFE

Too often, we associate joy solely with circumstance. Yet joy is a state that we can also create from within. We cannot do this, however, by ignoring or suppressing the uncomfortable. While it may seem somewhat counterintuitive, it is only by doing the kind of work outlined in this book—cultivating a new relationship with our emotions that allows us to truly feel and experience every one of them—that we actually rewire our neural pathways for joy. This is why developing this new relationship with our emotions is ultimately so important: it creates a stronger foundation for joy and fulfillment.

The reason for this is that the practice of dismantling the ego guard, which we have explored extensively thus far, is what allows us to soften into our emotions in general; it does not discriminate between emotions. Therefore, when we are guarding against uncomfortable feelings like anger, sadness, or fear, we are at the same time unintentionally and often unknowingly guarding ourselves against our own potential to experience joy as well. The reverse is therefore also true: when we are letting our guards down to soften into our uncomfortable emotions, we are also moving closer to *everything* inside the heart, including the potential for joy.

One specific and very important catalyst of joy that arises from this softened state is a deepened experience of gratitude. Gratitude, too, can only be truly experienced when the ego guard dissolves, and in turn, we can only really experience joy when we are able to authentically feel gratitude.

In recent years, *gratitude* has become somewhat of a hype word, often used in certain realms of more superficial self-care culture. And while trendy practices like gratitude journals do work, and there is a science behind why they work, it is important to recognize that genuine gratitude is never a forced experience. True gratitude arises naturally as we begin to move closer to our own hearts. As we drop the walls that guard us from feeling uncomfortable emotions, the disappearance of these walls gives way to more frequent experiences of genuine gratitude, and these experiences of gratitude give way to ever-increasing states of true daily joy.

This is the kind of joy that arises, sometimes, for seemingly no rational reason at all; it is a joy that is independent of external circumstance and experience, and is born instead of a vulnerable and open relationship with our emotions. When we prime our neural pathways for gratitude and joy in this way, we then begin naturally to focus on the daily experiences that bring us even *more* gratitude and joy, which then further enhances those neural pathways—and so the positive cycle goes.

And, just like with the nervous system rewiring of any emotional habit, to generate and experience this level of gratitude and joy on a regular basis actually requires some practice.

It is one thing to *know* in our minds what we are grateful for, but to practice fully *feeling* gratitude for these things is a true skill. It is a skill that takes cultivation and, most importantly, vulnerability. This vulnerability is, again, something that the ego mind typically tries, with good yet misguided intentions, to protect us from experiencing.

We all know what this ego defense feels like—when someone deeply thanks us or offers us a sincere compliment, for example, and we experience either a fleeting or strong sense of discomfort that usually causes us to brush off that person's words, rather than to receive them at the level of the heart.

Yet, to allow ourselves to receive so deeply that it invokes a visceral feeling, even if it is at first a slightly uncomfortable one, is to create powerful shifts in body and mind. To create these shifts, we must do more than simply think; we must *practice* the art of receiving, and of savoring what we receive. This is the art and the practice of genuine gratitude.

And when we allow this genuine gratitude to touch our hearts, truly savoring the things for which we are grateful, we consequently allow our internal barriers to dismantle. This, in turn, releases what is often a default subconscious state of inner withholding or bracing against joy; it thus opens the floodgates for joy to flow more freely through us, and to more readily inform our daily experiences, regardless of what is occurring in the external environment or circumstances.

To release this state of inner withholding, though, our nervous systems have to become accustomed to a new way of being. If we are not accustomed to fully showing up and being in relationship to others, ourselves, or life in that way, then it might take some time to truly engage in a practice of authentic gratitude and deeper receptivity. Because, as we know, our brains operate primarily via habituated patterns, and because we therefore always want to feel "like ourselves," even when that version of ourselves is not truly serving us, we have to actively and compassionately encourage our nervous systems to let these guards down so that we can soften into full receptivity—and then, furthermore, so that we can truly *feel* gratitude for that receiving. Because this is a shift that takes place at the level of the nervous system—just like with all the other exercises in this workbook—it takes time, practice, patience, and yes, most importantly, self-compassion.

Susan Kullman

BOX: PRACTICE & REFLECTION

The Art of Receiving and Savoring

You can practice the art of receiving and savoring all the time, with many, or even all, of the seemingly small experiences you encounter daily.

Below are a few examples to help you get started. The purpose of this exercise is to allow your nervous system the opportunity to calibrate to new vibrations of pleasure and desire. The following are only suggestions; you can allow your own self-expression to emerge as you tap into your personal sense of pleasure and savoring at the deepest possible level with each of these typical daily experiences:

- While taking a shower, see if you can more fully sense the water running down your back. Relax your body as if you are opening every pore of your skin. Can your body and senses truly *receive* the feeling of the water?

- Take an intentional moment to deeply experience your favorite food. Before you begin to eat, pause and notice the different aromas of the food. Close your eyes and see if you can detect what spices are present. As you begin slowly to chew, notice what textures and temperatures are available to your tongue. Pause and really experience this as you allow your body to receive what you are eating, and perhaps to feel gratitude for it.

- Take a moment, or several moments, during the day to just pause and smile as deeply as you can. Allow every cell in your body to open up and receive the warmth of your own smile.

- Look at yourself in the mirror with deep self-love —allow your heart to open fully, and allow through whatever expressions of joy and love may come naturally.

When you first begin this exploration, it is not uncommon to experience a sense of awkwardness, or thoughts that seem to question the significance of this exercise. You might even notice uncomfortable emotions arise, such as anger or frustration. Do your best, again, simply to witness these emotions without judging them or trying to push them away.

Practice patience through these potentially awkward first stages of rewiring your neurological pathways for joy, pleasure, and desire. Write down some of the elements of your experience with this practice.

GRATITUDE & WELLNESS

Just as shifting our relationship to our emotions can impact our physiological wellness in addition to our emotional wellness, more deeply experiencing gratitude also yields both emotional and somatic impact.

As we begin to rewire our brains for gratitude, we consequently also change the actual chemical reactions that occur in the body as a result of new thoughts. These altered chemical reactions allow the nervous system to move into a parasympathetic state, a shift often called *the relaxation response.*

Moving into the parasympathetic state of the nervous system has various positive effects on our bodies and minds. Physically speaking, it interrupts the production of a stress hormone called cortisol. Not only does cortisol increase our stress levels, it also causes inflammation in the body. Therefore, given that so many diseases are a result of inflammatory processes and generally heightened or imbalanced cortisol levels, a genuine and regular practice of gratitude can help us begin to literally shift the balance of our somatic experience of disease and wellness.

Furthermore, being in a parasympathetic state also increases other neurochemicals such as serotonin and dopamine, a task that also happens to be one of the primary functions of certain anti-anxiety and antidepressant medications. And while these medications are of course sometimes required to support a state of neurobiological balance in certain individuals, it is important to understand that we do often possess more power than we might think to also participate in the natural shift of our own neurochemical ratios, a shift that subsequently allows us to feel very differently in the world.

Generally speaking, most of us therefore wield the potential to play a more active role in changing the way we feel, both physically and emotionally, on a regular basis. By letting down the defenses that, since childhood, have been developed and strengthened in an effort to "protect" us from all that is uncomfortable or difficult to feel, we end up not only reaping the learnings and greater self-intimacy that arise from processing those emotions, we also consequently soften, without discrimination, into *all* of our feelings, including gratitude and joy.

As we focus more on these innately generated experiences, they begin to naturally occur with greater frequency, intensity, and duration—first internally, and then, as a result of this inner shift, they also begin to show up much more often in our external environments and circumstances.

Our heightened emotional awareness brings us greater choice (i.e., to focus on positively impactful emotions such as gratitude and joy), greater choice brings more abundant opportunities for personal empowerment, and when we practice that personal empowerment repeatedly, it eventually becomes integrated embodiment. This is when the cycle of *awareness to choice to empowerment* becomes second nature, and we are able simply to live it without exerting conscious effort.

And then suddenly, before we know it, through the power of our own active participation and courage, we have transformed.

BOX: PRACTICE AND REFLECTION

Gratitude

Write a list of at least twenty things for which you feel grateful, no matter how big or seemingly small. The purpose of creating such a list is to elicit a vibration of gratitude within, and simply to practice being with it. As you write your list, rather than focus too intently on the individual things you've written, see if you can allow the general vibration of gratitude to spread into every part of your mind and every cell of your body.

You can even choose to set a timer, and practice sustaining this feeling of deep gratitude for different amounts of time—beginning, for example, with just one minute, and working your way up to ten, or perhaps even twenty minutes.

Allow the walls that may have existed in the protective part of your being to come down slowly, and allow yourself to simply fall into a vibration of gratitude, love, and joy. As best you can, allow your body to receive and savor these vibrations completely.

Now, begin to physically move in a way that feels in alignment with these vibrations, and is deeply pleasurable for your body. Can you surrender so much in this moment that you actually begin to let your body tell you how it wants to move in accordance with the sensations of gratitude, love, and joy?

Then, reflect on and write an answer to the question:

What does this deep vibration of gratitude, love, and joy feel like in your mind, heart, and body? Describe it in as much detail as possible.

Do your best to make this exercise a daily practice, even for just minutes at a time if that is what feels comfortable and possible for you, and continue this practice until you feel able to surrender your guard long enough in order to receive these newly wired vibrations of gratitude, love, and joy throughout your entire mind and body.

Like everything else, even this requires practice and the awareness that it is an unfolding process, but eventually your nervous system will adapt to this elevated vibrational state as a new normal—a new, much healthier and more transformational "comfort zone."

As with every other exercise in this workbook, be sure to practice patience and self-compassion as you journey on this new path of growth and change.

Susan Kullman

THE ROAD AHEAD

Susan Kullman

I HAVE CHOSEN TO SHARE the information and practices contained within these pages with you because, throughout my fifteen-year coaching career and my twenty-five-year journey through personal evolutionary growth, I have experienced that the only thing standing in the way of moving forward with manifesting the heart's desire is the block we tend to create to fully feeling our emotions.

Therefore, making progress on the road towards personal growth, transformation, and freedom requires one critical thing: vulnerability.

To practice experiencing emotion at new levels will always feel vulnerable, and you will most likely have to surrender a deeply rooted belief system that desires "proof" of validity for the permission to feel what you feel.

Also, because of the temptation of the uncomfortable comfort zone to keep you trusting your old reference points of reality and identity, letting go of something that is so known, even when it no longer supports your highest wellbeing, will always create a feeling of vulnerability. This may feel difficult at first, yet it is this surrender to vulnerability that will open all the most important doors for you to move forward.

Since vulnerability is a state of heightened receptivity, the depth to which you can become vulnerable with your own emotions is the extent to which you will experience palpable transformation, both within and, therefore, in your external reality.

I would like to stress the point that absolutely anyone can do this; there is no one who, with willingness and the proper support and guidance, cannot become more vulnerable and feel more deeply, more authentically.

In fact, there is not a lot here to *do* in order to accomplish this. There is no need to become so caught up with all the "doing". The true source of our personal evolution exists within, and it always will.

Even if you were somehow to achieve the entirety of your ever-elusive "to do" list, you would still discover a remaining need to engage in the internal reconditioning of the mind in order to find true solace, peace, balance, and growth. It is through this positive conditioning of the mind that desired realities will manifest, and not the other way around.

This is why meditation and mindfulness are critical tools on the journey to self-transformation: their consistent practice results in heightened self-compassion and nonjudgment, which then reap a new set of distinct behaviors and results. These behaviors and results yield new habits, and these habits cumulatively generate a new reality.

To cultivate the skill of just feeling your feelings from a place of nonjudgmental awareness, rather than endlessly thinking about feelings, is one of the fundamental cornerstones of self-mastery and truly life-altering transformation.

My sincere hope is that you will apply the principles and practices in this workbook to positively shift your previously programmed beliefs, which may have thus far impacted your life in ways that do not best serve you or reflect who you are at your core, and that in courageously creating such a shift, you might unlock your innately unlimited potential.

And here, beyond the former threshold of what you had previously thought possible, you may find that you come face to face with a simultaneously more vulnerable, powerful, and radically authentic version of who you really are—now newly wired to embrace the entire spectrum of your own human emotions, and therefore capable of creating that which your fully feeling heart desires.

Susan Kullman

ABOUT THE AUTHOR

A certified spiritual self-mastery coach, somatic educator, and yoga therapist, Susan Kullman is the owner of Intentional Wellness and Yoga Center. Throughout her 30-year career of working with people in the various mind/body modalities, she has helped people achieve their own self-mastery by providing spiritual guidance, encouragement, and knowledge of mind/body connections.

Her passion comes from her own healing transformation. After experiencing illnesses and undesirable life events, Susan was faced with the challenge of healing herself physically, mentally, and psycho-spiritually.

Her journey led her to acquire a tremendous amount of knowledge and numerous accredited certifications in the alternative healing health field. Her continual thirst for knowledge of the mind and the body and how they are integrated into the universal unconsciousness comes from a true passion for the human Spirit and condition and quantum physics.

Having gone through all the aspects of her journey, Susan clearly sees the importance of the roles of both eastern and western medicine. It has become her personal mission statement to bridge the gap where traditional medicine leaves off and everyday life begins.

Born and raised in NY, Susan graduated from Ithaca College with a B.S. Degree in marketing management. She continues to enjoy yoga and dance as a way to continually practice the mind/body connection. Susan lives in New York with her husband Michael and son Jack.